SHOWING THE RIDDEN PONY

SHOWING THE RIDDEN PONY

A GUIDE
*to the Selection, Training and Production
of Ridden and Working Ponies
under saddle*

by

CAROLINE AKRILL

J. A. ALLEN
London

First published in 1981
by J. A. Allen & Co. Ltd
1 Lower Grosvenor Place
Buckingham Palace Road
London SW1W 0EL
New, revised edition 1990

British Library Cataloguing in Publication Data
Akrill, Caroline
  Showing the ridden pony. - 2nd. rev. ed.
  1. Livestock: Ponies. Training & care
  I. Title
  636.16

ISBN 0-85131-513-5

Typesetting and make up by
T & S Typesetting, 1 South View, Hewish, Avon.

Printed & Bound by WBC Print, Bridgend.

Contents

		page
	List of Photographs	vi
	List of Text Illustrations	vii
	Preface	ix
1	The Modern Riding Pony	1
2	The Working Hunter Pony	9
3	Type and Suitability	16
4	Conformation and Purchase	30
5	Feeding and Conditioning	43
6	Schooling	54
7	Show Pony Jockey	78
8	Saddlery for the Show-Ring	88
9	Grooming and Turnout	101
10	Ringcraft	121
	Addresses	136
	Recommended Reading	137
	Index	138

List of Photographs

                                                                  Page

Pretty Polly seen winning the Championship at
  Richmond Royal Horse Show in 1952   4

Holly of Spring 1976   5

Cussop Heiress with Carol Gilbert Scott   7

The working hunter must be a bold, careful performer   10

Pageboy ridden by Alison Bucknell   11

Hartmoor Silver Sand   13

Friar Tuck at Peterborough 1974   14

Example of pony with Welsh blood   19

Finer pony for a diminutive rider   20

Good type of 12.2 riding pony   21

Gem's Signet, a famous 14.2 riding pony   23

Lennel Aurora, many times a champion   24

Benedict of Rossall by Nutbeam Crispie   26

Blagdon Gaytime ridden and produced by Wendy
  Dallimore   28

Snailwell Charles ridden by Nigel Hollings   37

Coveham Fascination   38

Yeoland Foxglove   41

Novice ponies gaining courage and enjoying jumping   73

A nice hat is no good at all if the hair underneath
  looks awful   80

W.H.P. Champion Cawdor Helen and Jane Hankey   82

Perry Ditch March Winds   84

Carroll Cooper riding Centurion Minuet   85

Page

Carola Williams on Solway Sweet William 1972   96

Cantref of Glory ridden by Andrew Cousins   112

Do not jostle to get your pony into the ring first   126

A study in concentration   128

List of Text Illustrations

page

Leading Rein Combinations   18

Typical show ponies   25

The perfect specimen has yet to make an appearance   30

Ewe neck   31

Straight shoulders restrict movement   32

Examples of good and bad fronts   34

Examples of cow and sickle hocks   35

Dishing and plaiting   36

Correctly fitting lunge cavesson   55

Side reins fitted to the last girth strap   56

Sending the pony out   58

Pony creeping inwards. Opposite bend. Pony's quarters falling out   59

Side reins too loose. Side reins too tight. Side reins correctly adjusted   60

Good and bad outlines on the lunge   61

Walking towards the pony at halt. Coiling the lunge line   63

Working over trotting poles   67

Jumps for the working hunter pony   74

German eggbutt snaffle and Pelham bits   89

Working hunter pony tack   90

Bits for a double bridle   91

Example of a correctly fitting curb chain   92

Show pony tack   93

Pony dressed for travelling in cool weather   99

	Page
Studs for greasy going	105
Tail bandage	108
Tail plaiting	109
Natural and pulled tail	110
Plaiting the mane	116
Quarter marks	118
Your jockey should stand the pony up properly in front of the judge	130

Preface to the Second Edition

Almost twenty years ago, when I was the 'enfant terrible' of show reporters, I spent a lot of time at the ringside watching a lot of people making a lot of mistakes for want of a bit of timely advice. And I decided that, as life was short, and the time of life when one has the money, the energy and children of the right age for show ponies was particularly short, I would write a book filled with that advice – because the most valuable thing that learning from someone else's mistakes and experience saves, is time.

At that particular time of my life, the longest thing I had written was a magazine serial about showing (Stuart and Nigel Hollings used to read extracts to their long-suffering companions on the school bus which gives you an idea how long ago it was) and I felt my reporting career might soon be terminated. 'I have had cause to complain about your reporting before,' the formidable Glenda Spooner wrote, 'but your latest effort is more than any of us can stand and I have asked the Editor not to send you to any more of our shows.' So the time was ripe for a new project, and *Showing the Ridden Pony* was written.

Now, revising the book for the second edition, I am struck by the fact that although some things, like hoof varnish and the intermediate classes, are new, nothing has really changed. The showing enthusiast is still beset by the same problems; still undecided whether a rolled or a stitched noseband is best, still fretting about the lack of pony quality in the 14.2 classes, still grumbling about the judging, the entry fees, the prize money. Thus I hope this new edition of *Showing the Ridden Pony* will save both time and effort in a further generation of show pony enthusiasts. And I am pleased to find things so little changed. I would not have missed my years in and around the show ring for the world.

Caroline Akrill
1990

CHAPTER ONE
The Modern Riding Pony

If you asked a representative selection of the horsy public to give their opinion of the show pony, you would probably receive some rather rude replies. It could be said that the path of the modern show pony has been paved with the condemnations of its critics. Useless, ornamental, temperamental, in-bred; everyone has had a stone to throw along the way. Yet it is an indisputable fact that the show pony has been directly responsible for the tremendous improvement in conformation, quality and overall standard throughout the riding pony world in recent years. The show-ring is primarily the shop window of the breeder and the standard has never been as high. The backwash from the lovely exhibits paraded before the judges has been far-reaching. It has percolated from the show-ring, through the working animals, right down to the pony next door.

The chief accusation hurled at the show pony is that a practical, hardy, functional children's mount has been over-refined and made precious. All this is undoubtedly true. The show-ring specimen is not the animal you would choose to take your child hunting in plough country. This is not to say that he would not enjoy it, because he would. He would go like a bomb. In fact many of today's top show ponies can and do hunt. But it must be said that their perfection does inhibit their use. After all, a successful exhibit represents a large capital investment and most producers would no more use their ponies for hunting or gymkhana events than they would use their Crown Derby dinner service for a picnic.

To understand the relevance of the show pony, one has to seek a parallel in the horse world. Not everybody for instance wants, or could afford, the classic Thoroughbred horse. Yet most people want part of the legacy it can bestow in their own horses. They want some of the Thoroughbred's beauty, grace of movement, speed and courage. Similarly with the modern show pony, it is the diluted qualities which are so valuable. A tiny percentage in any kind of pony will make all the difference.

It is fairly certain that the modern riding pony would not exist at all were it not for the game of polo. The steady rise in the popularity of the game in the second half of the nineteenth century set a hue and cry for ponies of the right type. The scarcity of suitable animals was due to the fact that for generations the breeders had been striving to produce a taller Thoroughbred. They succeeded so well that the English racehorse was said to have increased in height by an inch every 25 years since 1700. Neither the small, tough, stocky native pony of the day, nor the tall, lightweight Thoroughbred with the startling turn of speed, were suitable mounts for polo. There was nothing in between. In an attempt to rectify the situation, the Polo Pony Stud Book Society was formed in 1893 and they set about trying to breed the ideal animal for the game. A polo pony needs to have quality, speed, courage and intelligence. He needs to be small, strong enough to carry up to 14 stone (89 kg), nimble, docile and have tremendous staying power. All this is a tall order but it was achieved by using the native pony as foundation stock, put to a small compact Thoroughbred or Arabian horse. Volume one of the Polo Pony Stud Book appeared in 1894 and contained the pedigrees and detailed descriptions of 57 stallions and 316 mares and their produce. This first volume contained details of ponies from all areas, excluding the Shetland, whose own Stud Book was already in existence. Subsequently the native ponies branched away to form their own societies and open their own registers. The Welsh came into being in 1901, the New Forest in 1906, the Dales in 1917, the Dartmoor in 1920, the Exmoor in 1921, the Highland in 1925, the Fell in 1927, and the English Connemara in 1946. It goes without saying that the first volume of any of these stud books is now almost a collector's item.

Thus the riding pony was born. The Polo Pony Stud Book Society is not the National Pony Society, whose sterling efforts to improve pony breeding through the exhibition of stock in the show-ring, through the education and encouragement of breeders and, more recently, through the approval and licensing of stallions, has set the pony world firmly on its feet.

Yet at the time many native breeders saw no future for the hybrid riding pony outside the polo field. They foresaw (and, it must be said, rightly) that the legacy of grace, speed, beauty and courage inherited from the Thoroughbred would bring its own problems. The pony would be too high-couraged for a novice, nervous or very small child. It wouldn't 'do' well and be able to live out all the year round. It wasn't weatherproof, or resistant to parasites. It hadn't the ability to 'browse' like a native and so could not survive on poor pasture. More important, it lacked the large percentage of native cunning, the instinct for self-preservation, that made the indigenous pony a sensible and safe ride across country, whether hacking, hunting or trekking. Lastly, even if the adage 'an ounce of blood is worth an inch of bone' proved true and the pony was capable of carrying an adult, its narrow lightweight frame would make it an uncomfortable experience compared with the armchair comfort offered by the native. But even with all these things against it, the riding pony found a ready market.

Like it or not, we live in an increasingly competitive age. Gymkhanas, show-jumping, eventing, hunter trials, long distance riding, pony club activities, almost every pony-owning child wants to take part. Our children demand ponies that gallop faster, jump higher, and have more courage and athletic ability than ever before. Add to this their preference for clean, stream-lined looks and it will be seen that the modern riding pony could hardly go wrong.

The early exhibition of the riding pony was a very haphazard business. Lack of guidance from a parent body meant that shows were left to work out their own classification and regulations, so that it was not unusual to come across classes for ponies not exceeding 14.3 hands to be ridden by persons under 21 years of age. Ponies were usually grabbed and measured before they entered the ring, which could be an upsetting experience.

The *coup de grâce* came when the winner of the class for novice ponies at the Royal Richmond Show in 1949 was discovered to be a well-known champion of previous years, piloted by a 'child' well over the age limit. This little débâcle set the showing world alight and the result was a meeting called by John Tilling, Brigadier Allen and Peter Knowland, at which 'Bill' Benson and Sir Berkeley Piggot represented the National Pony Society. Within a furious four hours of discussion the British Show Pony Society was born, a set of rules drawn up and a panel of judges nominated. However, when John Tilling and his wife wrote to the judges concerned, they were astonished to discover that they had been ostracised by 60 per cent of the horse world!

But the society survived. A hard core of loyal supporters spread the word by attending shows and persuading the

Pretty Polly, seen here in 1952 after winning the championship at Richmond Royal Horse Show, trophy presented by the Earl of Athlone. Polly was probably the most outstanding pony of her day and was partnered by Davinia Lee Smith and bred by the late Albert Deptford

secretaries to let them use the microphone. Before the start of the ridden pony classes, exhibitors were exhorted to join the new society and the opportunity to win a special rosette was offered as a carrot. It worked. Not long afterwards the Joint Measurement Scheme was introduced and exhibits no longer had to stand under the stick before each class. In that first year, the society had just 50 members. Today the membership of the BSPS stands at over 7,000 with a healthy growth rate.

Looking at photographs of champions when the British Show Pony Society was in its infancy, it is clear that the riding pony of the time was often a strange mixture of native pony, hunter, cob, Thoroughbred weed or freak. Yet there were some ponies of outstanding merit. Some had been brought over from Ireland and were to become the pattern of the future. Perhaps the best known of these was Pretty Polly, hard to fault even by today's demanding standards.

The modern riding pony is a magnificent success. From the Valentino–Pretty Polly line – Holly of Spring 1976

The best way to go about breeding the riding pony has always been a subject for endless conjecture and argument. In comparison, breeding the native pony would appear to be a fairly simple matter of putting the best mare to the best stallion, improvement of the breed going hopefully hand in hand with the retention of the particular characteristics which are the quintessence of the breed. But when the riding pony rears its head, everyone has their own pet theory, their own recipe for success. Riding pony people dislike the word hybrid. Yet for all that, this is what the riding pony is.

The one point on which everyone agrees is that the native pony is the heart of the matter. The fundamental native characteristics of hardiness, strength, honesty and true pony quality have to be retained and there is the need to fix the size. It has never been more important for a riding pony to look like one. Nobody (we hope) is trying to breed little horses!

The National Pony Society will accept riding ponies for registration provided that they are sired by an animal registered in the General Stud Book, the Mountain and Moorland Stud Book, or their own register, out of a mare to whom the same ruling applies. It will be seen from this that there is a lot of scope. In theory, a riding pony can be a small horse, an Arab, or a Shetland! In actual fact it almost never is. A pure bred native pony belongs to its own classification alone, and in the eyes of the pony world, without pony blood, there is no pony!

The riding pony is custom bred. The native pony (excluding the Shetland whose size and type make him unique but unsuitable) put to a small Thoroughbred, can breed a good type of riding pony, more so if the result is a filly and put back to the native. Possibly the best stallion to use on a native mare is the three-way cross, having a percentage of Thoroughbred, native and Arab blood. It is generally agreed that Arab blood, like salt, should be used sparingly. No meal should ever be without it, but add too much and the dish is ruined!

Sometimes, because a stallion is outstanding and throws super stock, he can become a cult, like Bwlch Valentino, who was by a Thoroughbred polo pony out of a Welsh foundation stock mare. In the ridden pony classes there have been dozens of ponies sired by Valentino or his sons, Zephyr and Hill Wind, and some of our finest ponies have come from the Valentino line. It is when ponies have the same blood on both sides, in the sire as well as the dam, that line breeding becomes dangerously like in-breeding and can eventually be responsible for excessive lightness of bone and congenital defects. I use Valentino as an example only to demonstrate how tempting it is to weaken a line by going on for too long on the strength of past success without an infusion of fresh blood from an outcross.

Many of the frail creatures which may be seen propping up the riding pony young stock classes are the result of zealous line breeding and they are the prime target for the critics. Yet it is only fair to say that not every painstakingly bred pony is a gem, and whilst every breeder breeds from the line and type of pony that he admires, he certainly does not admire every pony that he breeds. There is a strong element of chance in every match and one only has to look around to realise that even in the human race many a dud has impeccable parentage!

However, there is no doubt that the modern riding pony is a magnificent success. It is the ultimate in quality, grace, beauty, speed and courage. The temperament may be a bit high-powered

Full of quality and elegance, Cussop Heiress with Carol Gilbert Scott

sometimes but the breeders are not complacent; they will get it right in the end. The riding pony is the result of dedicated selective breeding over a long period of time but it has not been developed purely as an exercise in genetics. Nor has it been bred in order to provide a suitable mount for wealthy and indulgent parents to display their offspring to the crowd, although this is how other sections of the horse world often see it. Behind the satin rosettes, the silver trophies and the rather precious image there is something deeper, although the casual observer may have to scratch about a bit to find it. The purpose of the modern riding pony is to improve the ordinary pony for the ordinary child. That, rather than the trappings of glory heaped upon it in the show-ring, is its greatest triumph.

CHAPTER TWO
The Working Hunter Pony

The pattern of the riding pony has evolved over a good many years and it is a measure of its success that the front line in any show class is of such a level standard that judging is often a matter of personal fancy. To the ringside observer the exhibits look identical and their minor flaws and differences are only discernible to the dedicated enthusiast.

As yet, this has not entirely happened in the working hunter pony classes, even though they are overflowing with entries. But it is still early days and it may well be another decade before a level standard is achieved. All things considered, it is not surprising that the pattern has taken even longer to emerge than that of the show pony. The chief reason for this is that the requirements for a working hunter pony are even greater. Allied to the standardisation of type, the working hunter pony must have performance. He needs to be clever, willing, bold and agile, as well as kind, free-moving, beautiful, fast and substantial, all of which is not achieved in five minutes. You may be sure, though that the pony world is working on it. The working hunter pony can be a straight cross between the riding pony and a native (Welsh, New Forest, and Connemara are much favoured), a native crossed with a small hunter type, a riding pony of a more substantial type, or a pure native. It is a type rather than a breed, and it was not until 1985 that the Hunter Pony Stud Book Register was founded by Susan Thorne to promote the breeding of the working hunter pony to a suitable pattern. Subsequently the register was taken under the wing of the NPS. The ideal working hunter pony has the looks and substance of a small hunter, the performance of a working hunter and the size and quality of a pony. The main criterion is that he should be a suitable animal to carry a child in the hunting fiend. He should also be schooled and obedient and his paces should be straight, sound and correct. He should not display the extravagant movement of the show pony but his gaits should be long, level, smooth and free because short choppy paces are undesirable in a hunter. He should have a swinging, active walk, a long-striding, regular trot, a comfortable balanced canter and a naturally long, low gallop.

Over fences, the working hunter pony must be a bold and careful performer

Over fences, the working hunter pony must be a bold and careful performer, clever enough to get himself and his charge out of a sticky situation, easily controlled and able to perform at a good hunting pace. Conformation-wise, he will be heavier than the show pony in every way. He will have more bone and substance, a plainer head and have a more workmanlike appearance and action. He should not be pretty but he must not be coarse. He must be handsome and personable because if he is to be truly successful in the ring he must have the quality and presence to set him above the crowd.

The advent of the working hunter pony has meant that the pony world has had to look to its stock and its future. The pony societies are encouraging shows to stage classes for working hunter pony youngstock and these are filling up with some impressive exhibits, some of which are likely to become the champions and foundation stock of the future. There are now studs catering expressly for the demand for the working hunter pony, and established riding pony studs have expanded in order to breed both types. Already the best of the winning ponies are

Ideal type of pony for the 15hh working hunter pony class, displaying boldness, substance and quality and still recognisable as a pony. Mr and Mrs J. Bucknell's Pageboy ridden by Alison Bucknell

beginning to rival the riding pony in value and there is little doubt that they will eventually overtake it. But there is no danger that the riding pony will become obsolete because when the hue and cry over bone and substance in the working pony class has reached its logical conclusion and the pattern has become a miniature cob, it is to the riding pony that the breeders will return to regain a measure of lightness and quality. This is by no means to denigrate the cob which has many fine qualities but does not have the speed, agility, courage, quality and staying power so essential in a hunter.

There is still a fair amount of criticism to be heard at the ringside of the working hunter pony classes, sometimes about the points system of judging, sometimes about the unsatisfactory courses provided for the ponies to jump, but more often about the eventual winners that are placed, and even some eventual champions have not, conformation and type-wise, been everyone's idea of the perfect working hunter pony. Yet the winners have always been true performers in every way even if they have not looked the part; and performance, in a working animal, must be the deciding factor; thus the less than perfect pattern does often win over its better endowed counterpart. This happens all the time in working hunter classes, horses and ponies alike. Everyone hopes that the faultless pattern with performance to match will win, but everyone agrees that the faultless pattern is useless if it does not perform!

In time, with ponies custom bred and schooled for the class, the standard will doubtless become very high indeed, at which point the inferior animals will be squeezed out. This will be a great shame in a way, because the strength of the working hunter pony classes at the moment is that everyone feels that they are in with a chance. Huge entries and great enthusiasm may create judging, space and time problems for shows, but there are a great boost for the pony world and they bring showing, hitherto a rather select and introverted affair, within the reach of a wider section of people. This cosmopolitan effect is to be encouraged at all costs. The showing of ridden ponies could be considered as art, but the showing of the working hunter pony is quite definitely sport and it generates a warm-hearted infectious atmosphere, a spirit sometimes sadly lacking in top class riding pony competition, where the championships are often battled out in grim silence between a few leading professional stables, whilst the owner/rider/producer combinations look wistfully on.

The Working Hunter Pony Class was discovered by the late Keith Lee Smith when he took a team of our best show ponies and riders to compete against their American counterparts. They were astonished to discover that the Americans expected their show ponies to perform over fences! The British contingent, after some hasty schooling, scrambled over as best they might. Rather to everyone's surprise, they acquitted themselves very reasonably and enjoyed themselves so much that on his return Keith Lee Smith discussed with Mrs Glenda Spooner (founder of the Ponies of Britain, and an entrepreneur if ever there was one), the possibility of trying a ridden pony class catering for a more workmanlike pony, to be judged on performance as well as suitability and looks. Mrs Spooner subsequently initiated the Working Hunter Pony Class at her Ponies of Britain Show.

About this time, the British Show Pony Society were casting about for a new class to allow the rider with a more utility type of pony to compete in the show-ring, and in 1969 a small committee was formed to look into the possibility of staging a class to include some jumping, based on the American idea.

A year later, 38 shows staged a working hunter pony class under the umbrella of the BSPS and 66 winning ponies competed at Peterborough for the first ever championship. The society readily admits that the advent of the working hunter pony gave the showing world a boost when it was in danger of becoming stagnant, and is largely responsible for making the BSPS the lively and flourishing body it is today.

There were teething problems of course. The class was, and indeed still is, very time-consuming and difficult to judge, involving two separate phases and a complicated system of points. Some early shows had quaint ideas of what constituted a suitable obstacle for a working hunter pony to jump – they either

This photograph shows the solid construction of the type of obstacle a working hunter pony can expect to meet at the BSPS Championships. The pony is Hartmoor Silver Sand

borrowed a few striped poles from the show jumping arena, rolled in a few bales of straw, or, in an effort to be creative, terrified exhibitors with arrangements of conifers and artificial grass borrowed from the local greengrocer.

To rectify the situation, the BSPS briefed shows and judges and brought out an illustrated sheet which pointed out that fences should be as natural-looking as possible, constructed of solid, rustic materials, and not easily dislodged. Amongst the examples optimistically included was a Pytchley Ditch consisting of brush or faggots on the take-off side, guarded by a six-inch-thick rustic pole, sited in front of a dug-out ditch of sufficient proportions to give any dedicated groundsman a heart-attack. Few of the chaste showgrounds of England approved the Pytchley Ditch, but courses improved noticeably after the appearance of the leaflet.

No mention of working hunter pony courses would be complete without reference to Mrs Davina Whiteman's Championship courses at Peterborough. They are an object

Friar Tuck meets the plastic ducks, Peterborough 1974

lesson in course building and whilst it is well nigh impossible to reproduce the hazards of the hunting field within the confines of a show-ring, the course is natural, substantial and testing, and always includes a few surprises. There have been bridges, fords, towering bullfinches, open ditches and trappy combination fences. One year the water jump was alive with plastic ducks which daunted all but the brave, but provided excellent spectator sport!

Not surprisingly, in the initial stages the class was over-run with failed show ponies and sub-standard show jumping ponies who saw it as their salvation. Because a lot of exhibitors and even some of the judges were not too sure what qualified as a working hunter pony, the judges at the first championship were faced with a somewhat mixed bag. They managed to find a worthy champion, however, in Diana Clapham's 13.2 hands bay gelding, Tonto. Tonto was that rare creature, the ideal pattern with the performance to match. He became the mascot of the working pony world and invariably received a rousing cheer whenever he appeared.

The championship show at Peterborough is an essential pilgrimage for the working hunter pony enthusiast. It is an education to see not only hundreds of prize-winning animals, imaginatively constructed fences and the following that the class has gained in its first two decades, but also to realise that the working hunter pony has done more than anyone would have dreamed possible to put the fun and sportsmanship back into showing.

CHAPTER THREE
Type and Suitability

If you are just idly considering the possibility of buying a pony to produce for the show-ring as a hobby, my advice would probably be 'don't'. Insanity, bankruptcy, divorce and worse lie in wait for people who dabble in show ponies. It seems unbelievably eccentric that people will spend whole fortunes and use up lifetimes in pursuit of little bits of coloured ribbon. Yet they do, and most are as sane as you or I.

If your mind is made up however, I can offer three main pieces of advice. Decide exactly what your requirements are before you set out to buy, look at lots of ponies before you finally choose, and buy the best pony you can possibly afford. The last piece of advice will probably make you blanch and I am not saying that there are no bargains to be found but the truth of the matter is that good ponies are very expensive to breed and it makes sense to spend a little more on the initial purchase when you consider that a winner costs the same to keep, enter and transport as a loser, with the added bonus of a little success now and again. By that, I do not mean that you should go out and buy a champion, because if you spend a fortune on a pony who has already reached the top, he has only one way left to go – down!

You should certainly shop around within your price range. Because you cannot buy ponies with the quality labelled, and sold by the pound like tea, what you get for your money varies, according to the optimism of the vendor. If you are an absolute novice, determined to buy the best, the only thing to do is to put your faith into one of the top professional producers and ask them to find a pony for you. You will have to pay a commission on the purchase but you will almost certainly be found a good animal because the professional has a reputation to protect. He is also in the centre of things and may have at his fingertips the one pony you might have travelled the length and breadth of the country to find. The top professionals often get the pick of the best ponies from the riding pony studs simply because the breeders know that their stock will be expertly produced and have every chance of getting to the top, thus creating valuable publicity.

Personally though, I feel it is far more fun to find your own pony and learn from your mistakes, even if some lessons are hard learned. The first thing to do if you are setting out on your own is to study the class you are aiming to exhibit in. Take yourself to as many shows as you can, the bigger the better, and fill your eye with the very best. Then make a study of your own requirements and the requirements of the class. This should give you a fairly clear idea of what you should be looking for. Height classification as set out by the British Show Pony Society has a lot to do with the type of pony you will require and the classes and their requirements are set out below. All classes are for four years and over, apart from Novice classes as stated.

Leading-Rein Ponies
(Pony not to exceed 12 hands. Rider 7 years or under. Sometimes divided into not exceeding 11.2 hands and not exceeding 12 hand sections.

Not everyone realises that the size of the child should dictate the size and type of pony you should buy, because the overall picture you present to the judge is of paramount importance. If you are buying the pony first and are then able to find the jockey, this may not apply, but if the prospective jockey is your own child, you are, if you will forgive the expression, rather stuck with what you have and the size of the child is the prime consideration. A pony up to the height limit for instance, will look like a Shire if the jockey's feet barely reach the saddle flaps. A miniscule rider on a large pony is delightful in a Thelwell cartoon, but it will not do at all in the show-ring, where points are gained or lost on suitability.

A tiny child will need a very small, narrow pony which will very likely have Welsh or Dartmoor blood. The pony should be pretty and dainty and it should have smooth, comfortable gaits rather than darting extravagant action, which can upset, or actually dislodge a tiny rider.

A large child will need a bigger pony, and if his legs are long, it will be an advantage if the pony is also wider, thus avoiding having to let the stirrup irons down to the level of the pony's knees; or worse, making the child ride too short.

A tiny child is not expected to be very much more than a passenger enjoying the ride, but the older child is expected to be a little more competent and the pony must respond to the

Leading Rein Combinations

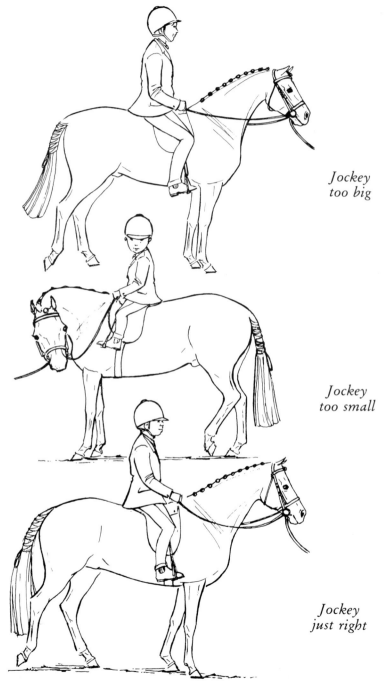

*Jockey
too big*

*Jockey
too small*

*Jockey
just right*

Chunky pony with obvious Welsh blood compliments rider – and handler!

jockey's aids. Some judges ask the rider to dismount and lead the pony a little way to prove that it is suitable for a child to handle and will not take off like a rocket as soon as the leader lets go of the rein. Larger children may be expected to mount unaided to display that the pony is patient about it, and all this must be considered when selecting a leading-rein pony.

It stands to reason that the manners of the pony should be impeccable, but to be a success the pony should not be a slug. The ideal leading-rein pony is perfectly tailored to its rider, is willing, well-mannered, obedient, beautiful, relaxed and inspires everyone with confidence. These very small ponies show their native blood very strongly and rightly so. Miniature riding ponies are unsuitable for the class because they are likely to be too fast and high-couraged for the tinies. That is not to say that they do not sometimes win! Judges have personal fancies. Some are enchanted by the tinies, others go for the bigger, more eye-filling combinations. Some like a particular colour, some have a breed prejudice. Personal fancy though, as I have said before, only comes into it when the judge is faced with several ponies of a level standard and all judges worth their salt insist on good manners, smooth steady paces and suitability in a leading-rein pony.

First Ridden Ponies
(Pony not to exceed 12 hands. Rider 9 years or under.)

A leading-rein pony is by no means a first ridden pony as well; although some do compete in both classes, the majority stick to their own side of the fence.

As in the previous class, suitability for the rider will dictate the size and, to some extent, the type of pony required; and as the child will be unaccompanied in the ring, the temperament and schooling are very important.

Pay no attention to the school of thought which demands that you buy a pony right up to the height limit on the grounds that it will fill the judge's eye much better than a smaller pony, who might look more suitable for the Leading Rein Class. The only criterion for the height of the pony should be the size of the child and if your child is small, do not be tempted to overmount him.

Finer pony, dainty and narrow for a diminutive rider

A good little one is every bit as good as his larger counterpart, probably better, in view of the smaller, younger, less experienced child he has to look after. Again, the first pony will not be a miniature riding pony, he will show obvious native blood and may be pure native. He must be, and look, a safe, confidence-giving conveyance, as befits a pony that will give the child his first taste of riding alone. So the elegant little pony, teeming with quality and looking for trouble, will not do at all.

What the judges are looking for in this class is a nice-looking little pony, showing plenty of native blood, not too sharp but by no means a stubborn little slug, that does willingly everything his rider asks him and *nothing more*. One sees a lot of ponies in the class just being steered round, but the child must be seen to be in control and to have to ask the pony to do things. Therefore a pony that hangs back slightly is a better first pony than one that is more intelligent and anticipates, ending up one step ahead of the jockey. A really good first pony is one of the most difficult things to find.

Good type of 12.2 riding pony – rather swamped by the rider which unbalances the overall picture

Riding Pony not exceeding 12.2 hands
(Riders 12 years or under)

The fact that most children of 12 or even 11 years are too hope-lessly large for a 12.2 pony does not enter into it at all, so if your jockey is very tall the best advice I can give is to hop straight up into the 13.2 class, rather than jeopardise your chances with an unsuitable combination.

Once you reach the 12.2 class, you are in the realm of the riding pony, so the chubby little native will not do at all. Nevertheless, it is generally agreed that the 12.2 pony should show more native blood than his larger counterpart. He should, though, show far more quality and be much more free-going than a first pony; he will also be finer.

The 12.2 pony is expected to give a much more sophisticated display than the first pony and this usually includes a gallop. It stands to reason that manners are high on the list of require-ments in this class because whilst a judge may forgive a tiny bit of exuberance in a 14.2 with which the older, more experienced child should be able to cope, it will not be forgiven in the 12.2 because of his younger rider.

Riding Pony exceeding 12.2 hands, not exceeding 13.2 hands
(Riders 14 years or under.)

The 13.2 class often contains the finest examples of the riding pony. At this height the exhibits are large enough to fill the eye, they and their jockeys are capable of giving a polished and sophis-ticated display, they are full of quality and elegance, yet they are small enough to retain their pony character. Even in the riding pony classes the combination element should not be overlooked as a very small or over-large rider can present an unbalanced picture to the judges.

Riding Pony exceeding 13.2 hands, not exceeding 14.2 hands
(Riders 16 years or under)

It really is difficult to find a good type of 14.2 pony, because so many are hack or hunterish. When the demand for larger polo ponies led to the height limit being increased from 14 hands to 15 hands, there was an immediate outcry from the pony enthusiasts of the day. The late Reggie Summerhays deplored the fact that the change let the small Thoroughbred into the game. 'It is to be

The 14.2 Conundrum (1) Gem's Signet, a famous 14.2 riding pony by Bwlch Hill Wind. A lovely animal beautifully produced, full of quality but rather 'horsy'

hoped', he commented, 'that once again we shall see the game played on animals of pony height and true pony character.' The NPS warned breeders against using big Thoroughbred stallions in order to produce larger ponies. 'Even if the produce of these is right,' they said, 'the next generation may be either a child's pony or a hunter.' One has only to be at the ringside during the judging of a class of 14.2 ponies, to realise that the problem is still with us.

I really cannot stress strongly enough how absolutely essential it is that the 14.2 exhibit shows true pony character. One often hears people saying that the modern riding pony should resemble a miniature hack, but there is one all-important difference and that difference is pony quality. No judge would want to see obvious pony blood in a hack and it is just as important that the riding pony judge should recognise that a miniature hack without pony blood should not be able to win a pony class. With the introduction of the Juvenile Riders' class, the ideal opportunity has arisen for judges to be far more insistent on true type in the 14.2 class and some show signs of doing so.

As befits a larger pony suitable for a teenager to ride, the 14.2

The 14.2 Conundrum (2) Lennel Aurora by Lennel Strolling Ministrel. Many times a champion and a true pony in every way

should be a free-going, bold and balanced ride. He should show that he is well able to gallop and satisfy the demands of his more experienced rider, but he should remain calm, well-mannered and obedient. He should not hot up, neither should he look as if he lacks enthusiasm. Of all the ridden ponies, the 14.2 should be the one that the judge would most like to ride.

Novice Ponies

The classification is usually the same as the other pony classes. Three year old ponies can be registered after 1st June and may be shown after 1st July. The definition of a novice is not having won a first prize of £5 or over at an affiliated show, thus a pony who has not won this at 1st October 1990, is eligible as a novice until 30th September 1991 regardless of how many novice classes it may win.

Typical show ponies

Leading rein

Riding pony

Working hunter

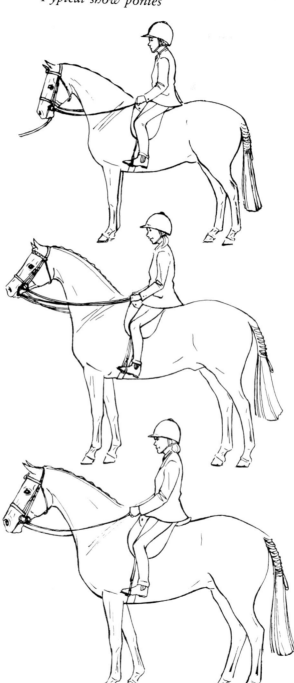

Riding Pony exceeding 14 hands, not exceeding 15 hands
(Riders 18 years or under)

In 1969 the BSPS introduced a new class for animals exceeding 14 hands, not exceeding 15 hands. This was seen as a stepping-stone to assist the young rider to make the transition from pony to hack or hunter show classes. It has proved very popular, providing a niche for the overgrown pony or the undersized hack who can still show some pony quality.

Working Hunter Ponies
(Up to 15 hands)

The requirements of the working hunter pony have been discussed in Chapter 2 and they are the same, whatever the height of the pony. Naturally it is important that he is the right size for the rider and temperamentally suited to the job.

A successful child's first pony who went on to be a champion working hunter pony. Benedict of Rossall by Nutbeam Crispie

The working hunter pony needs to be bold and free-going, but an excitable temperament is undesirable because the perfect hunting pony should never hot up. It is just as important that the pony should enjoy jumping and even if the pony is novice and unshown, the prospective purchaser should ask to see him over some fences, even very low ones. Rushing and over-enthusiasm in a young pony can often be corrected with time and patience but do not buy a pony that jumps reluctantly, refuses or runs out. An experienced person can school or force any pony to jump, but no power on earth can make him enjoy it and this will always show in his performance and when the pressure is on, he will always let you down.

Show Hunter Ponies
(Classification as Working Hunter Ponies)

What the judges are looking for in these classes are miniature hunters with pony quality. One needs to get in one's 'eye' by watching the open hunter classes, to develop an ability to scale down one's requirements without losing the performance and manner of going, and pony quality *is* important, never more so than in the largest height class. The ponies should be ridden, not like show ponies, but like show hunters, they should gallop well, be bold but biddable.

Essential Considerations before Purchase

Apart from conformation, which is so complex that it has to have a whole chapter to itself, there are other important considerations to think of before selecting a suitable animal.

First of all, a word about temperament, which quite honestly can be a matter of life or death to the person on top, or occasionally, underneath. If you think this is black humour, let me tell you that it is not, it is *deadly* serious!

The point I would make is that you should never consider buying anything but a pony with a friendly, obliging nature. Bad-tempered ponies in the hands of children are lethal and terrifying. Do not buy a meanie either. A generous pony will always give his best and he is very easy to love. He will often be placed above ponies who are far more stunningly beautiful to look at, simply because he has played his part and is anxious to please. But a little sourpuss who throws away your precious chances time after time because he looks miserable and will not try for you, will break your heart.

Another point is that if you have a nervous or inexperienced jockey, it is a mistake to buy a promising youngster on the hopeful assumption that you will all learn together. More likely, you will ruin the pony and the pony will frighten you and your jockey to death. It is far better to buy an experienced pony, past his best, who really knows his job. I say 'he' because most good mares retire to stud after their successful years in the ring, but geldings tend to go on for ever. This veteran 'school-master' will teach you and your jockey confidence and ringcraft. What is more, he will not be too expensive and after he has taught you all he can, he will be easy to pass on to another novice newcomer, that is, if you can bear to part with him. After that, you can go ahead and buy your promising novice.

In conclusion, the pony must be selected to suit the class, the rider and the family. Suitability, temperament and good

Nicely presented pony in a side-saddle class showing neat plaits, clear quarter markings and 'dragon's teeth'. Blagdon Gaytime by Bubbly, ridden and produced by Wendy Dallimore

manners are as important to the show pony as the most astonishing good looks. It is foolishness to over-horse a jockey, because even a well-schooled animal will start to misbehave if he senses that he can get the upper hand. You will achieve nothing if your jockey is unnerved and once a pony gains a reputation for being naughty in the ring it sticks with him all his days, affecting not only his showing career, but his value.

It is well to remember that showing, unless you are a breeder or a professional producer, when your life actually depends on it, is entered into for fun and enjoyment. An obvious statement perhaps, but a very easy one to lose sight of.

Side-Saddle, Pairs of Ponies, Teams to Music

These classes will normally fall into the usual classification of height and age. Side-saddle ponies need a good front and long, smooth gaits.

CHAPTER FOUR

Conformation and Purchase

Good conformation is universally important. Bad hocks, for instance, are just as undesirable in a leading-rein pony as in a heavyweight hunter, so the following pages are relevant whatever kind of pony you may be looking at.

It must be said that the best way to get an eye for good and bad points is to study the show classes themselves, preferably with an experienced person to guide you. By the time you have compared the end-of-the-liners with the winners and studied hundreds and thousands of ponies, you should be able to pick a winner and you will also have discovered that even the winners have their faults. The perfect specimen has yet to make an appearance. Also there is the human element to consider. A long, swan-like neck may be seen as an advantage by one judge and as an abomination by another and these slight differences in opinion are the reason why many exhibitors 'pick' their shows carefully according to who

The perfect specimen has yet to make an appearance

30

may be judging. On the whole, the fact that all judges do not think alike is very right and proper, otherwise if everyone felt the same way, the results would always come out the same and after the first few shows, there would be small point in exhibiting again.

Bear in mind that the study of conformation from a book can be no more than a starting point. At its worst it is a mystery not even fully comprehended by the writer; and at its best it is a bore, and I have faint hope of improvement!

To start from the most attractive end, the head should be small and neat, and viewed from the side, the line from the poll to the muzzle can be straight or slightly concave (as in the Arab) but it should not be convex. A roman nose is all very well on Julius Caesar but on a pony it denotes common blood.

The eye should be large and kindly as opposed to small and piggy, and the ears should be small, sharp and neat. The cheek bones should have cleanly defined curves and when the pony flexes (bends from the poll) the glands should slip neatly behind them, not stick out as if the animal has had an attack of mumps.

A short, thick neck may be ideal for ploughing or trekking in Snowdonia, but it will not do in the show-ring. Ponies with thick necks find it difficult to flex properly because they are also thick through the jowl. This means that they go along looking as though they have swallowed a broom handle and they invariably give the impression of being too strong for their jockeys, even if they have good mouths. A good length of neck is essential because it helps the rider to feel secure in the saddle. Nothing

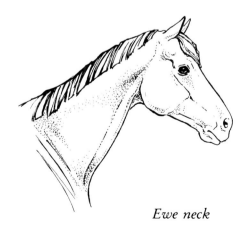

Ewe neck

Straight shoulders restrict movement

feels worse than sitting on a pony whose ears are only inches away from your own. A good length of neck, though, must not be 'ewe' shaped which is an upside-down effect caused by the lower line (from breast to jowl) being more pronounced and muscled up at the expense of the top line. Generally the working hunter may well have a shorter, thicker neck than the show pony; this is excellent as long as it is in proportion to the rest of the body.

It is easy to imagine that because a pony has a good length of neck, it has a good front. But a good neck is useless if it is attached to a straight, upright shoulder. Straight shoulders restrict movement and a good shoulder is often referred to as 'well laid back'. This means that the shoulder blade (the scapula) is flat and sloping up to an elegant and well-defined wither. If the shoulder is lacking this clean, pronounced line and looks instead as if it has been stuffed with kapok, giving a heavy, lumpy appearance so that it is impossible to see the line of the scapula or the withers, this is known as a 'loaded' shoulder.

It stands to reason that a riding pony should have a deep chest (known as having plenty of heart room) and a good girthline. This is easy to detect if you imagine the pony wearing a saddle and means that the line under the belly in front of the girth should not rise upwards towards the chest. The line should always be deeper in front than behind. This is a practical necessity because if you had a pony with a poor girthline you would never be able to prevent the saddle from slipping forward.

An overlong back and a slack loin are signs of weakness, whilst a goose rump (prized by the show-jumping fraternity as a 'jumper's bump') spoils what is cherished by showing people as a good top line. A good top line is vitally important in a show animal and it means exactly that, the line from poll to tail. You can imagine what a catastrophic effect a ewe neck, long back, slack loin and goose rump would have on this top line, and whilst muscle can be built up by judicious exercise and strapping, one can never alter basic faults in conformation.

Neither can one do anything about a tail which is set on too low; this really can ruin a pony's looks. Likewise it is also important that a pony carries his tail properly. If a show animal goes around with his tail clamped uncompromisingly to his rump it is a disaster, but whilst one wants to see gay and natural carriage, a high, Araby, flag-flying tail is an embarrassment. The best place to assess natural tail carriage is when the pony is at liberty in a field.

Good sound strong limbs are clearly vitally important, and all joints should look hard and bony. This may seem a silly thing to say, but what I mean is that there should be no tendancy to roundness and puffiness. Sometimes you see ponies with joints that look as if someone has been round them with a bicycle pump. Knees should be flat and well-defined, cannon bones should be short, and you should be able to see the tendons standing out like cords: clean, cool and strong. Fetlocks should look clean and hard, pasterns should be short and sloping, not long and straight. Feet should be well-shaped and open, not narrow and boxy like a donkey's. Frogs should be well-developed, whole and clean-looking, not shrivelled, or soft and smelly. The horn of the hoof should be free from cracks and ridges. Hooves which are patterned like a beach at ebb tide are suspect as the pony may be prone to laminitis.

Viewed from the front, the forelegs should look straight. They should not be bowed or splayed and there should be a good width across the chest. If the chest is too narrow, the pony will be described as having 'both legs coming out of the same hole', but if he is voluptuously wide and a bit porky, he is 'bosomy' and that will not do either.

Something else to guard against is that the pony is not 'tied in at the elbow'. The accepted test for this is to slip a few fingers in between the pony's elbows and his ribs, and if you can get them in

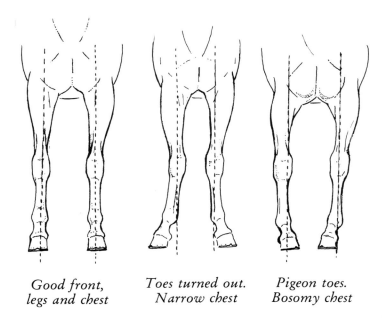

Good front,
legs and chest

Toes turned out.
Narrow chest

Pigeon toes.
Bosomy chest

all well and good. Putting this test into practice, I do not think it all that reliable as I find I can get a fist between some of my ponies' elbows and one of them who appears to have the freest elbow is the worst mover of all! I think that if a pony is really tied in, not only will you spot it in the action because he will not move well, but it will give a tendency to turn his toes out. Obviously toes that turn in or out as opposed to being straight are undesirable.

Hindlegs are the engine room so they should be well made and strong. Viewed from the back the quarters should look nicely rounded with a well-developed (less so in a youngster) second thigh. The hocks should follow a straight line, vertical to the ground; they should not point inwards towards each other like a cow. Over-long cannon bones denote weakness and viewed from the side, when the pony is standing up properly, they should be vertical, not at an angle to the ground, known as 'bent'. The overall line of the hindleg should not be too straight as this inhibits movement, but neither should it be too curved between hock and buttock.

When a pony is said to have so many inches of bone, the measurement is taken just below the knee. An exaggeratedly small

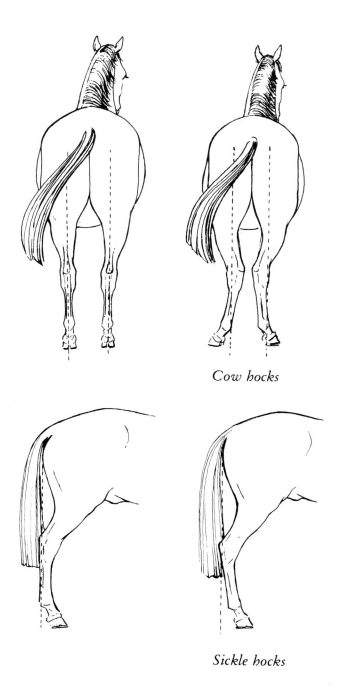

Cow hocks

Sickle hocks

measurement here means that the pony is 'tied in below the knee', which speaks for itself. Ponies that are very light of bone like this usually have other conformation defects and the cause is often inbreeding.

Bone is more important to the working hunter pony because he is expected to have plenty of substance, but when looking at the riding pony, one must take care not to mistake lightness for weakness. The old adage 'an ounce of blood is worth an inch of bone' may have become a cliché but it is true for all that. The riding pony is supposed to be 'fine' which may be explained as meaning light, elegant, refined and full of quality. In this respect then, lightness is all very proper but the important thing to remember is that *within the proportions of this fineness*, the conformation must still be right.

Movement

Movement is largely dictated by conformation. Rudolf Nureyev would not be where he is today if he had bow legs, splay feet and weak ankles, and the same applies to show ponies. If everything is in the right place it is reasonable to suppose that the pony will be able to move correctly.

It is fairly easy to develop an eye for correct movement. If you

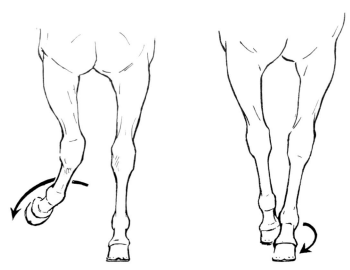

Dishing and plaiting

position yourself in front of the pony and have him trotted towards you in a straight line, you can see at once if he throws a leg out of true or interferes with himself in any way. He should move absolutely straight, not too close (the result of a narrow chest and poorly developed hindquarters), and not too wide, which looks hideous. Having ascertained how the animal moves from the front, remove yourself smartly from his path and watch him trot away from you from behind. What you are looking for now is to see that the hindlegs are also moving in a straight line and not plaiting along, and again that they are neither too close nor too far apart.

The next thing to do is to have the pony walked and trotted past you so that you can view it from the side. Watch now to see if the pony moves lightly and easily across the ground, particularly at the trot, that he gets his hocks well under him and uses his shoulders to push out his forelegs in a long, low movement. He must not trail his hocks, pound along with a lowered head so that

Extravagant action. This photograph really shows what a good shoulder is capable of. Snailwell Charles (by Bwlch Valentino) ridden by Nigel Hollings

A fine, close, glossy coat. Coveham Fascination

it looks as if he is 'going into the ground', or lift up his knees like a carriage horse. He should have naturally balanced carriage. If you watch the pony trotting free in the paddock, you will probably find it easier to make up your mind what kind of picture he presents and what his natural action and carriage is. Faulty action, balance and carriage can certainly be improved upon but it is obviously a very much easier task to produce a pony who is right from the start.

Once in a blue moon, you might find a pony who has perfectly natural extension and elevation. This means that he has the ability (and the conformation), to really engage his hocks and use his shoulders in order to fling out his front legs in a lovely long action with just a slight moment of suspension before the foot hits the ground. This is a delight to watch, and expert schooling can produce it. Overdone, however, it can look artificial and mechanical, and I know that many judges are just as happy with a pony that moves freely and correctly in a rhythmic and balanced manner. Extravagant action like this is often a disadvantage in the leading-rein pony and is certainly undesirable in the working hunter pony, and anyone who has hunted a pony that persists in demonstrating his brilliance knows why!

Two elusive extras essential to success in the ring are quality and presence. Quality, applied to a show pony, means that the animal appears to be well bred. The Thoroughbred characteristics might be said to be the hallmark of quality. A fine, close, glossy coat with little extraneous hair on the throat and heels, a straight silky mane and tail, an air of refinement, all these may be defined as quality and the introduction of Thoroughbred blood into our ponies gave all these things and more.

Presence is personality and *élan*. It is pride and gaiety of spirit, and it captures the eye and the heart of the onlooker. Unfortunately for the novice producer, not only the best ponies are blessed with it. Often quite experienced people, even judges, can be so blinded by the presence of a pony that they quite overlook its defects. Be sure though, that any success with a pony that is merely flashy will be short lived.

Veterinary Considerations

Never, never should the novice producer try to save a few pounds by not having the pony he is intending to purchase examined by a veterinary surgeon. It is true that most people, once they have gained an eye for conformation, can spot the knobs and twiddly bits on the legs that should not be there. Some splints for instance, are big enough to hang your hat on. But there are all manner of complex things that the eye cannot hope to see: heart tremors, wind complaints and sight problems, for example.

When you have found your ideal pony it is in your own interest to engage the very best horse specialist that you can find, even if you have to pay travelling expenses on top of the normal fee. This is your insurance policy. I do stress that you must engage your own vet and not be persuaded to use the vendor's own man and you must send a specialist. A farm vet or a city man who specialises in gerbils and budgerigars simply will not do the same job. When the certificate arrives, let it make up your mind. Any unsoundness is clearly undesirable in a show animal. Splints, curbs and other enlargements, hard or soft, may be curable, but they do denote weakness and animals with such defects are best left alone. It is sometimes agonising to have to turn down a pony you have set your heart on, but it is foolish to take a chance with your investment.

When the vet is examining the pony, be sure to have the pony measured, even if he has a life certificate issued by the Joint Measurement scheme (see Chapter 10). There have been a few cases in the past when ponies have been objected to in the ring by someone who suspects the pony is over-height for his class. If such an objection was made to your pony, he would have to be remeasured and if he was found to be even a fraction over the top, he would be 'measured out' and would never be allowed back into the class again. It is obviously heart-breaking to be measured out of the class by a hair's breadth when the pony has been purchased in good faith, so the purchaser of a pony who is well up to the height limit needs to take extra care. The tragedy of being measured out of a class is that each class has its subtle differences and it would be a disaster to be measured out of the first pony class, because the 12.2 riding pony is a different kettle of fish altogether. Not all ponies that turn out to be over-height have been fiddled through the system: some ponies are late to develop, others grow half an inch for no reason at all!

If the pony you are buying is registered as a riding pony or a working hunter pony you will be given its registration papers detailing its breeding, breeder, past ownership, description and stud book or register number. These will be issued by the

A pony that will give you pleasure. Yeoland Foxglove

National Pony Society. If the pony is a native, the papers will be issued by its respective breed society, for instance the Dartmoor Pony Society, or the New Forest Pony Society. The papers are your only proof that your pony is registered and of its breeding, and they will be very valuable to you if the pony is a mare or filly and you intend to breed with her later on. Mare or gelding notwithstanding, you should never accept a pony as registered without the accompanying papers. These should stay with the pony for all of its life. Do make sure also, that the description on the papers tallies exactly with the pony that you are taking home. It is not very likely that you would be sold a 'ringer' but it has happened!

It goes without saying that all the other golden rules of purchase still apply when buying a pony to show. You need to know if it is well mannered in the stable; good to show, trim and clip (especially if it is a working hunter pony and you expect it to hunt); quiet in traffic, alone and in company. Find out if it is good to load and travels well. Travelling is a large part of showing and it is no earthly good buying a pony which has qualified for Wembley if you have to ride it there.

Find out as much about the pony from the previous owner as you possibly can. Obviously it helps to know the pony's past stable routine, its likes and dislikes, quirks, what food it is used to, how much exercise it has been given, and what its previous showing record is. If possible, speak to a disinterested party who knows the animal. You will soon discover that if the pony is known in the show ring, other exhibitors will waste no time in telling you if it is naughty, nappy, sour or dangerous!

Once you have purchased the pony, you would be well advised to insure it and its equipment. There are insurance companies who specialise in equines and offer special rates if you are a member of a recognised body such as the NPS or BSPS.

In conclusion, after considering all the points set out in the last two chapters, it is essential that you buy the kind of animal that you like *personally*, a pony that will give you pleasure every time you look at it, because a lot of the time it will be only you who is looking at it. One of the few things you can guarantee in the show-ring is that whenever your exhibit is performing beautifully, the judge will have his back towards it!

CHAPTER FIVE

Feeding and Conditioning

Show ponies are roughed off at the end of the season and turned out for a good rest. It is amazing how even the most refined animal quickly reverts to nature, growing a thick coat and generally looking like nothing on earth.

Ponies wintering out need shelter and daily attention; it is not just a case of pushing them into a field and forgetting all about them until the spring. A south-facing open shelter is ideal and if there are one or two ponies out together, it must be large enough to minimise the danger of a shy animal being kicked. Narrow doorways or any kind of doorway to a shelter are undesirable because of kicking and because the 'boss' pony can actually prevent the others from entering. An open end is far better.

The ground inside a shelter soon becomes poached, so siting is important with regard to natural drainage. Otherwise a base which is dug out, filled with large stone, topped up with smaller stone, covered with 3-4in (7.5-10cm) of peat and woodchip with a bed of straw on top of that will need no further attention, apart from a skip out and half a bale of straw now and then. Dry ground which is well drained needs only a good deep bed of straw to be suitable.

Ideally, a pony needs 2 acres (8,000 sq m). Often, I know, he is lucky to get one. One acre per pony, though, is the bare minimum and, naturally, it must be well fenced. Post and rail fencing is perfect but frighteningly expensive. Thick, stoutly set posts and galvanised plain wire make a good substitute. Barbed wire is to be avoided at all costs. There is nothing better than a good thick hedge; it provides an excellent natural barrier, shelter from the weather, and once it has been well cut, the pony will keep it in trim by nibbling. I know people who use electric fencing and find it very effective for dividing a field but I doubt if it is suitable for a permanent fence.

Good grass management is very important to the basic health of your pony and whether you own or rent your grazing, it will repay you dividends if you look after it. Ponies dislike tall dry grass and the best way to get good grazing is to keep mowing it, never allowing the grass to seed. Young short grass is sweet and contains double the nutrients of grass which has ripened. On a farm or a large acreage, it is often possible to graze cattle and sheep after ponies, but this is not ideal as even they prefer the short grass and won't eat the rank until the rest of the pasture is bare.

If you only have a small paddock, mowing is easily done with something like an Allen scythe, but if funds will not run to such a machine, a hand scythe on the rank patches will do almost as well. Do remember to remove your mowings, don't pile them up to get hot and give your pony colic. Pick up droppings daily if at all possible, otherwise regular harrowing is essential if you are not to have dark sour patches all over the place. Well-grazed land gets hungry and old cattle manure is ideal for use as a top dressing. If you can't bear the thought of it (it shouldn't be slimy or liquid and it *is* cheap), buy a few bags of powdered fertiliser from your local supplier and spread it by hand from a barrow. (These self-sufficiency tips are aimed at the person with 1-2 acres only!) Fertilise your grazing in the late spring and keep your pony off it for at least three weeks. Provided that you have a little patch elsewhere to give your pony some freedom each day, you can take a crop of hay off your paddock in early June which is well worth having as even 2 acres will give you 60-80 bales. If you don't know a farmer who will bale it for you, or want to save money, cut and turn, sheaf and stook it yourself! It is jolly hard work but I have some friends who did just that and had the most beautiful long sweet hay for the winter. You must cut it before the seed heads open and make sure that it is absolutely dry before storing.

Worming should be carried out religiously every six to eight weeks. It is quite useless to worm once and then forget it. Honestly, you may as well not bother. Make a note on your calendar and stick to it.

Roughed-off ponies are best without shoes. You must always have them taken off by your farrier, not just wait until they fall off. Cracks and broken feet take ages to get right again. Probably once during the winter you will need to call your farrier to tidy up their feet with a rasp, and ponies with dodgy feet might be better shod with a grass tip to keep the foot from spreading. Your farrier will advise you.

Ponies need access to clean fresh water all the time. Tanks should be cleaned out regularly and inspected daily. For some reason birds manage to fall in and drown and they can pollute the water. I once found a baby owl floating in mine. Do make sure that there are no sharp edges or protruding bits around the tank. If there are you can be sure that your pony will knock a piece of skin off his face or worse. A few barrow-loads of shale or stone round the edge of the tank will help prevent it becoming a quagmire.

Personally, I feel that a pony with some native blood and a good coat, provided that he has shelter, has no need of a New Zealand rug. He will certainly be more comfortable without. New Zealand rugs are ideal for a clipped animal or for use during a cold or wet spell during the show season, but in the winter when nature has provided a woolly coat for the animal's protection they do prevent it from doing its job properly by flattening the hair which should actually stand out and hold a layer of warm air for insulation. Also, if they do not fit properly they rub withers and shoulders, chafe legs, and slip round when you are not looking. My own ponies are not rugged at all, even in the most severe winter.

Some producers bring their animals in at night all through the winter and this has the advantage of personal contact. The top door of the stable should be left open and the pony can wear a jute rug. Thorough grooming, though, is out, because the dirt and natural grease should stay in the coat for insulation. It is advisable to groom well where the roller lies because dirt here will rub and cause galling, but only a flip over the rest of the coat is permissible.

Tiny native ponies often do so well that they can winter out with not much more than a wedge of hay when the ground is frozen, but ponies with a bit more Thoroughbred blood need a feed every day and hay as well. There is no hard and fast rule for winter feeding because each pony is an individual and must be fed as such. In the winter your pony needs to be 'soft' fat, which means you feed as much natural food as possible. Flaked maize, sugar beet, bruised or boiled barley, linseed (cooked!), bran and cod liver oil are ideal. The value of roots should not be overlooked. You may be able to buy a trailer-load of carrots fairly cheaply after Christmas and they are a welcome addition to the diet. Watch your pony like a hawk, because when he comes in he needs to be well fleshed if he is to maintain condition all through the season. You will only create problems for yourself if he becomes gross, or at the other extreme, poor, during the winter.

If a working hunter pony is expected to hunt during the winter and show during the summer, there must be a break of at least a month in between. Hunting condition is not show-ring condition and the pony will need to let down and put on a little soft fat before the shows begin. He also deserves a holiday!

Most show ponies are in by February, some by January and a few are even in by Christmas. Again, this all depends on how easy the pony is to produce and there is no hard and fast rule. As soon as the pony is in, ask your vet to come and run his fingers along his back teeth. If there are any sharp edges, have them rasped down. This looks terrifying and the noise will make your hair rise, but it is not as bad as it looks and ponies do not get as upset about it as you might think. Teeth are the main cause of problems like head-shaking, yawing and quidding (dropping little balls of food), and the latter can cause loss of condition. A sharp edge beneath the noseband, especially with a leading rein attached, can cause a riot and be put down to temperament – some people do not even realise that ponies have teeth that far up!

If your pony has been wintering out, especially with cattle, give him a de-louse before he comes in. You can buy a large drum of louse powder and you should sprinkle it lavishly all over the pony, paying particular attention to the roots of the mane and tail. He may need two, or even three applications – you may even need one yourself! Most horses and ponies have a few lice in the spring and they really do make them itch, resulting in patches of rubbed skin and ruined manes and docks.

After any lice have departed, put your pony in his stable. There is not room here to go into stable construction, but yours should be light, well ventilated and draughtproof and it must be large enough. 10ft by 10ft (3 x 3m) is a good size for a pony up to 12.2 hands. 10ft by 12ft (3 x 3.6m) is better for anything larger. Concrete is the usual flooring for a loose box but it does have the disadvantage of being much colder than the old brick floors. A thick layer of peat under the straw is a good idea, because if you are trying to get a coat through or put condition into the pony, it must be kept warm. Stuffiness, however, is not warmth, so do not close the top door – a deeper bed is a much better idea. When you are mucking out, scoop up the sodden patches of peat and rake the lower surface level. The peat and the dirty straw can go on the muck heap together, they will make your manure more saleable. Some ponies tend to eat their bedding, especially if they are on a diet. In this case it is better to bed them on peat or wood-chips instead. Peat and woodchips come in large bales. Wheat is generally considered to be the best straw for bedding.

Water should be available to the pony at all times and there should be a mineral lick or rock salt both in his stable and in his winter field shelter. You will still need your paddock because ponies get bored standing in the stable all day, so it is advisable to turn them out for a few hours, more especially if they have not been out for some exercise. A New Zealand rug will be invalu-able to you now because you must keep him rugged in order to get rid of the shaggy winter coat. Loose blankets under the New Zealand rug will be a disaster, but a lined jute rug will stay put. A few hours of freedom each day will pay dividends in keeping your pony sweet tempered.

Schooling comes into the next chapter, but exercise is quite a different matter. I think it is very important that show ponies should Get Out and See Life. I know only too well that all the life many see is the schooling paddock and the show-ring and I regard this as a deprivation which so often results in a sour, stale and ruined animal. Owners must obviously work out their own routine which will depend on the time and facilities available and also on the pony.

The tiny ponies are often shown unshod and if the feet are hard and sound, there is no reason to have shoes on at all. But even tiny ponies should do some roadwork and if necessary your farrier should fit steel tips or light steel shoes to prevent the pony becoming footsore. Alloys (aluminium shoes) are ideal for the ring, being feather light, but they will not last five minutes on the road. If you like your ponies to do a lot of roadwork, ordinary shoes may be used and normal weight shoes should always be used for working hunter ponies.

Tinies do not need to be very fit, because over-fitness in the ring can cause problems in a class which consists mainly of walking and standing about. The easiest ponies to produce are those which can be turned out all day to exercise themselves and just be given one period of walking exercise and one of schooling each week. There are many tiny ponies who thrive on just this and they are a godsend to the producer.

Small ponies doing roadwork are usually led on foot and they should be in tack, meaning a bridle, roller (or saddle), and side-reins. It is no earthly good leading out a pony in just a head-collar because you will not have enough control and he will learn bad habits like grabbing at roadside grass when you are not looking. Side-reins are best when they have elastic inserts to provide 'give' and guard against a dead mouth. They should not be tight at any time and should be positively loose to start with. As the neck muscles gradually become accustomed to the discipline of side-reins, you can begin to shorten them to such a length that will encourage (but not enforce) a correct and steady head position. (More about side-reins in the following chapter.) You will find that leading your pony out 'in tack' makes him pay more attention, carry himself properly, and step out better, and you will be in full control.

Try to vary your roadwork each time you take your pony out and show him every aspect of life that you possibly can. Traffic, children's playgrounds, roadworks, farm animals and even funfairs, all of these should be part of his education if it is at all possible. A county show, after all, is one huge farm and funfair combined. Include gradients in your roadwork because they are invaluable for muscling up poor quarters. They also encourage your pony to use his shoulders and get his hocks under him. The best way to teach a pony to walk out properly is to get him going downhill and then try to maintain the impulsion on the flat. Be sure that the pony walks almost an arm's length away from you and carries himself. There is nothing worse than a pony that walks on top of you. Another point is that it should be you, not the pony, who sets the pace. You must teach him to keep up, walking with his shoulder level with yours. This is dealt with in the next chapter and it is very important because a pony that either hangs back or drags you along will be a disaster in the show-ring. All ponies love to go out. New sights and sounds are a stimulation and an education. Exercise is far better done like this than in the paddock where the pony becomes bored and uncooperative.

Larger ponies can be ridden out and if possible they should sometimes go alone, and sometimes in company. Exercising alone helps to combat nappiness but if you always exercise alone you may find your pony becomes excited when you do take him in company. Again, the same principles apply. It will do the pony no good at all to slop along the same old ride time after time. He should step out properly and you should vary the rides as much as you can. With a soft pony, start with 15 minutes' walking exercise and build up slowly over three to four weeks to about an hour and a half (three-quarters of an hour is usually enough for a tiny being led in hand, unless the leader is very energetic). Trotting should be introduced gradually at first because jarring will cause strain and sprain to slack muscles. Always trot along at a slow, regular pace and as the pony gets fitter, the periods of trotting should get longer. I know that some people who produce ponies will not necessarily agree with all this emphasis on road work, but I think that if you only work on the soft, you are inviting trouble later on. In a normal summer there will be days when the ground is like iron and a show pony needs to be as hard and as constitutionally sound as a hunter to complete a full season.

Whilst we are talking about riding ponies out for exercise, a word regarding safety. Recent statistics show that one out of every six riders on the road will have a hair-raising experience sooner or later. This is not heartening news, and there are things you can do to lengthen the odds. One of the primary considerations is a sound knowledge of the Highway Code. The main thing to remember is that you must always keep to the left-hand side of the road. Grass verges can be a blessing, but look out for drainage ditches and other hazards which can be hidden by long grass, and never take your pony across a mown frontage which someone obviously regards as part of his garden!

If you have to lead another pony, always keep it on the near-side, and if you are leading on foot, place yourself between the pony and the traffic. This may confuse a leading-rein pony at first but he will soon get used to it and it is a great advantage to be able to lead from either side, not only for convenience but because it helps to keep him going forward in a straight line, not bent towards the leader.

Make sure also that you are covered by insurance for third party liability because if you fell off or let go of your charge who took off and caused an accident, you could be sued for substantial damages. This happened to me when my over-fresh hunter jerked his rope out of the hand of his attendant whilst being led from field to stable. To everyone's horror he bolted straight up onto a main dual-carriageway and was hit by a car. The horse recovered but the driver sued for damages. My insurance company fought the case and won, but I would not have been so successful on my own. These days, both the police and insurance companies would probably hold the horse owner responsible for any damage caused by a loose horse.

The BHS have two useful little leaflets which they will send you for the price of a stamped addressed envelope. They are 'The Safety Code for Riding' and 'The Riding Code'. They also have another leaflet called 'Riding and Roadsense' which is published by the Royal Society for the Prevention of Accidents.

Feeding

Feeding is a complex subject and everyone you speak to seems to have different ideas. Again there can be no hard and fast rules because the type of food you give and the number of times a day you give it, depends entirely on the requirements of the pony.

Provided that the pony has no weight problem, hay should be available to him all the time. It is most important to feed only the very best hay. It should be a year old: clean, hard and sweet. Musty, dusty hay that is over-soft is just a waste of money. I like good meadow hay, but others like seed hay just as much, so it is really a matter of personal choice and also, of course, the pony will probably decide for you. It is obviously better to feed him what he likes best. For ponies with respiratory problems, Horsehage is excellent. Some yards dunk all their hay in a big tank then hang it to drain before feeding to avoid dust.

Hay chop makes a marvellous base for feeds, especially if you can chop it yourself because bought hay chop tends to be made from inferior hay and sweepings. At the risk of beginning to sound like a self-sufficiency manual, it is perfectly possible to cut your own chop even without a chaff cutter. All you need is a strong pair of scissors and endless patience. When I had two tiny leading rein ponies I used to spend hours in the barn with the bacon scissors, snipping hay into a bucket, and I found it extremely therapeutic!

Chop is a very good mixer and it prevents ponies from bolting their feeds. Many people use it instead of bran, which is no longer the quality that it used to be. Sugar-beet pulp is another good mixer and ponies usually love it. It comes either flaked or in cubes and it must be soaked, preferably overnight. The flakes must be soaked in $2\frac{1}{2}$ parts water to 1 part flakes; the cubes must be soaked in 4 parts water to 1 part cubes. Then you scoop it out, juice and all and it damps the feed at the same time. Be sure to keep it cool and covered and make it fresh daily as it tends to ferment quickly. Chop, sugar-beet pulp, carrots and first class hay is a good diet for a tiny who tends to be a little fatty and does not need any heating, high-energy food. You could also give a little linseed jelly, or linseed oil, once a week.

As a general guide for the larger pony who is expected to do more work, to the basics of chop, beet and roots, you could add some high-energy food. Oats are generally considered to be the best food a horse or pony can have but they are very heating and a corned-up pony can so easily lose its manners. Some ponies, though, do not give of their best without them, and if this is the case you can count yourself lucky and feed him all the oats he needs. You can feed them bruised or boiled. If oats cause your pony to lose his head there are plenty of substitutes. Micronised, flaked or boiled barley, flaked maize, or pony nuts all make good substitutes. Barley and maize are very good for keeping condition on a pony as are milk pellets which are completely non-heating. Pony nuts seem to me to be surprisingly high-powered but despite careful examination of their listed ingredients, I have never been able to grasp the reason why!

Linseed is rich in oils and very good for the coat. It should be cooked and fed as a jelly, but not more than once or twice a week because it does have a laxative effect. For two ponies, put $\frac{1}{4}$ lb (113g) of linseed in a pan and cover it generously with cold water. Leave it to soak for 24 hours, then bring it to the boil and simmer very gently, adding more water if necessary, until the seeds are completely soft and have sunk to the bottom of the pan. This takes several hours and it smells awful. When the linseed is cool it will set into a jelly which can be added to the feed. Linseed doesn't keep, in fact it becomes toxic rather quickly, so don't cook more than you can use at one time. If you can't bear the thought of cooking it, buy linseed oil and add a tablespoon to the feed once or twice a week instead.

Boiled barley is slightly less complicated as you just fill the pan half full of whole barley, cover it generously with water and boil until it swells up and splits. It should be soft when squeezed between thumb and finger. You can add a tablespoon of salt if you like. Boiled barley is very good for a poor animal.

Standard stable routine used to dictate that all animals were given a bran mash the night before their day off for the good of their health. Some people still follow this rule and swear by it and if the pony is having a lot of corn and you can get decent broad bran, it certainly does no harm. One top show stable gives a sort of bran-based pudding the evening after a show. Barley and linseed are left slowly cooking all day and are made into a bran mash on your return from the show. The time it takes to steam allows the ponies to settle down after the journey and a hot feed like this is certainly very comforting after a hard day. To make a bran or pudding mash, scald however much bran you need in a bucket with boiling water or your boiled pudding, adding more boiling water if necessary in order to make the bran really wet but not a sloppy liquid. Add a little salt if you like, stir well and cover with a sack until cool enough to feed. Bran is very useful to use as a mixer if a pony tends to be constipated. If the droppings are small, hard and dark use bran as a mixer and damp his feeds well: this will have a laxative effect. (Normal droppings are light chestnut in colour, slightly glossy, an oval shape and soft enough to break when they hit the ground.)

Many people feed extra vitamins and supplements and everyone you talk to swears by something different. In moderation, feeding a good multi-vitamin supplement is a good idea, but it is not a substitute for selecting only foodstuffs of the very best quality, storing them well and feeding them correctly.

The number of feeds you give per day can only depend on the pony and the amount of work he is doing. A little fatty who is not doing very much at all can often get by on one solid feed a day, given in the evening. He can have hay in the morning and if he can spend most of the day out in a rather bare paddock, so much the better. A larger pony in regular work needs two or three feeds per day and a poor animal may need four or even five feeds per day until it gains the right amount of condition. Bear in mind that it is most important to keep a poor or shy feeder interested in his food – variety is important and lots of little feeds are preferable to a few terrifyingly large ones. Never feed a pony more than it will eat in one go and never leave loose food containers to be kicked around the stable. One of my ponies threw her food around so much that in the end we used to feed her from a baby's plastic bath. This worked very well until we forgot to take it out of the stable one day and returned to find her standing with her foot through the centre of it. She had turned it upside down and tried to stand on it, her hoof had gone through and it had fixed itself round her fetlock like a grotesque over-reach boot!

If a pony has wintered rather too well and comes in looking gross, then obviously he will have to go on a diet. You will find that 'soft' fat will vanish almost overnight, but solid rolls are quite another matter. Small feeds, very little hay and gradually built up periods of exercise are the answer. If the fat is very stubborn, you could try putting a polythene sheet over a rug on the fatty part to encourage sweating during exercise. You can actually buy neck and jowl sweaters to do the same job but whichever you use, do beware of chafing and heat-soreness. If a pony has a thick neck anyway, the only thing to do is to show the animal with less condition all over, taking care to keep it fit and well. Exercise, diet and strapping can work wonders, but not miracles.

It is advisable for ponies travelling to shows to have a 'flu jab. Some shows, like the Horse of the Year and Royal International won't let your pony compete unless they have a valid certificate. It is wise to organise boosters early in the year through your vet and keep the vaccination certificate handy, making sure there is an ID card for each pony.

When you reach the end of the season and the pony is no longer working, begin to rough off gradually by knocking the high energy food out of his diet and removing the under blankets one at a time. Choose a nice day to turn your pony out 'in the nude' for the first time, and for the first week at least, bring him in at night and put on a jute rug. This interim period will give the coat time to open out for insulation, to thicken, and to build up natural grease and dirt for added protection. Because of the latter factor, you should discontinue grooming, but make sure that there is no solid dirt under the roller area, which could chafe. Again, choose a mild night on which to leave the pony out altogether, after which he should be perfectly able to stay out all the time.

CHAPTER SIX

Schooling

The important thing to remember about conditioning a soft pony is that you must bring him into work slowly. You cannot ask very much of slack muscles and if you try to whiz off a few figures of eight straightaway, you are asking for trouble. Proper schooling cannot begin until the pony is well into regular exercise which means that he has worked up from 15 minutes walking exercise to about an hour and a half of steady walking and trotting (see previous chapter). Part of this exercise will probably be road work, the rest may be slow and steady work on the lunge.

Proper work on the lunge is invaluable for conditioning and suppling a pony but it must be done correctly. If you have no experience of lungeing, do take yourself off to one of the better equitation establishments and ask for lessons, because a lunge line in inexperienced hands can be a disaster. You see the most amazing sights at shows, where the most lovely ponies are being chased around at breakneck speed at great danger to life and limb in an effort to 'wear them out' before the class. Presumably the person in the middle hopes that the unfortunate animals will be too tired to do anything but behave. In actual fact, this kind of lungeing has the reverse effect b ecause chasing a pony round in circles does nothing but excite it and helps make it fighting fit – thus worsening the situation.

At its best, lungeing helps to calm and balance a pony and makes him obedient to the voice, which is a great asset, especially with smaller ponies. The value of lungeing an animal before he goes into the ring is that steady work on the circle has a soporific effect. It helps to make him relaxed and obedient and gets him into the right frame of mind, often difficult in new and exciting surroundings. Flogging an animal round and round at speed has the opposite effect because it stirs him up, so lungeing must be properly done to be of any value at all.

The modern lightweight cavesson is ideal for lungeing as it fits under a bridle. The old-fashioned variety is too heavy for a pony and in the past many people preferred to use a headcollar instead. A headcollar, though, does not give enough control, so invest in a lightweight cavesson if you possibly can.

Correctly fitting lunge cavesson

To tack up a pony for lungeing, put on a snaffle bridle minus the noseband and reins. Then add the cavesson and buckle the noseband under the cheek pieces of the bridle so that it will not interfere with the action of the bit. The cavesson should be fitted lower than the normal noseband to aid control but not so low as to restrict the pony's breathing or to trap the lip between bit and noseband. The jowl strap should be done up firmly because it prevents the cheek pieces from working round to the pony's eyes. If the cavesson has not got a jowl strap, the throat lash will do the same job but it should not be so firmly buckled.

One can argue forever about the value of side-reins but there is no doubt that they are very useful for lungeing ponies if they are used correctly. They should only act firmly on the mouth if the pony gets his head too high or too low, thus preventing him from yawing and grabbing at grass. Thus they can help to keep a pony straight and encourage him to seek contact with the bit. As mentioned previously, the best side-reins have elastic insets to avoid a 'dead' contact.

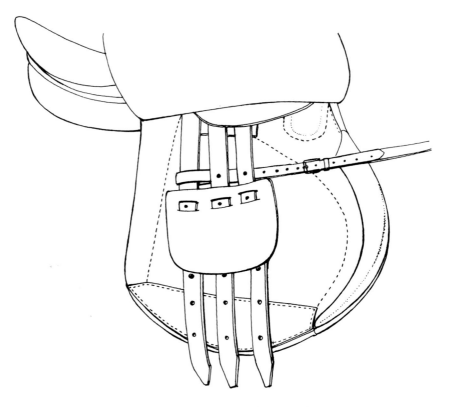

Side reins fitted to the last girth strap

The trouble with side-reins is that they are often misused by people who imagine that their purpose is to fix the pony's head in the correct position and force him to accept the bit. This never works and instead it has the reverse effect. If you adjust the reins so tightly as to impose an artificial position, not only will you cause pain in the pony's muscles, but also resistance, stiffness, and evasion, resulting in a hollow back and ruined mouth and action.

Ideally, the side-reins should be attached to a roller, but if you do not have one, a saddle will do. If the pony is rather round you will also need a crupper, because otherwise he can yank the roller or saddle forward onto his shoulders. To fit the side-reins clip them onto each side of the bit and buckle them onto the roller. If you are using a saddle, slip the loops through the last girth strap (nearest to the cantle) and buckle the other girth straps over the rein to help prevent it slipping down. The reins should be quite loose when starting with a soft pony and should not do anything except remind him that he is on the lunge to work, not to take a mouthful of grass whenever he feels like it. As the lunge periods progress, the reins can be gradually shortened to provide a gentle contact, with the inside rein one hole shorter to give a hint of the correct bend you expect on the circle.

The buckle of the lunge rein should normally be attached to the front ring of the cavesson because this affords more control, but a tiny light pony may find this too heavy and if he begins to resist and obviously finds it so, it is better to buckle the lunge rein to a side ring instead. You will need a long lungeing whip to keep the pony from creeping in towards you on a smaller and smaller circle, and to maintain the impulsion. You may also need brushing boots, over-reach boots, or bandages – this depends very much on the pony, his action and behaviour on the lunge. Some producers insist on boots and bandages for lungeing, some do not. It is up to you. You, yourself, should wear a hard hat and gloves.

Most ponies have been lunged as part of their basic training and they never forget, so you are unlikely to have any trouble. The first time you may like to have an assistant who can lead the pony to the outside of the circle. After that, it should only be necessary to point the whip at the shoulder, give an allowance of rein and say 'Out' firmly, to start the pony off.

You should begin by lungeing in large circles (about 66ft/20m) because small circles are tiring for slack muscles. The pony should work steadily in the 'V' made by the lunge rein and the whip, which should be held pointing just behind his tail. As the pony moves round you will need to turn yourself in order not to be unyielding, but you should not move about too much because the pony must remain on a regular-shaped circle for the exercise to have any point. You sometimes see lungeing being done so sloppily that it is difficult to see who is getting the most exercise, the person or the pony!

The purpose of lungeing is that the pony should maintain smooth, even gaits on either rein, learning balance and obedience, developing free forward movement and suppleness, improving his action and building muscle in the right places. It is most important that the pony should learn to bend correctly from the

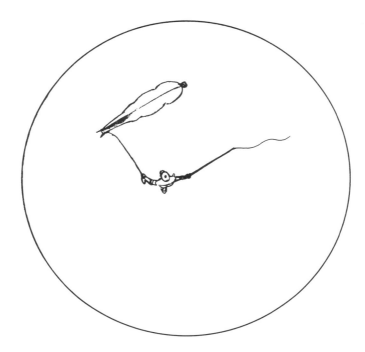

Sending the pony out

very start. He must bend round the circle with his whole body, not just his neck, which is a very common fault made worse by lungeing in too small a circle, by tightening the side-rein too much on the inside, and by too much work on one rein only.

It is obviously most important that the pony is worked equally on both reins but if you find that he goes very much better and bends correctly on one rein and not the other, you will have to concentrate on the bad side until the situation improves. Always do some work on both reins otherwise you may encourage the reverse situation, but work longer on the bad side. Start with large circles because the fact that the pony goes so badly on the one side means that he has not had enough work on it to develop the correct muscles and become supple and this can only be corrected gradually. It is no use at all trying to take short cuts by lungeing in small circles and tightening the side-reins on the inside as this will only make matters worse. Steady, patient work on a large circle, gradually decreasing the size as the pony gains elasticity is the only answer and you have to accept the fact that,

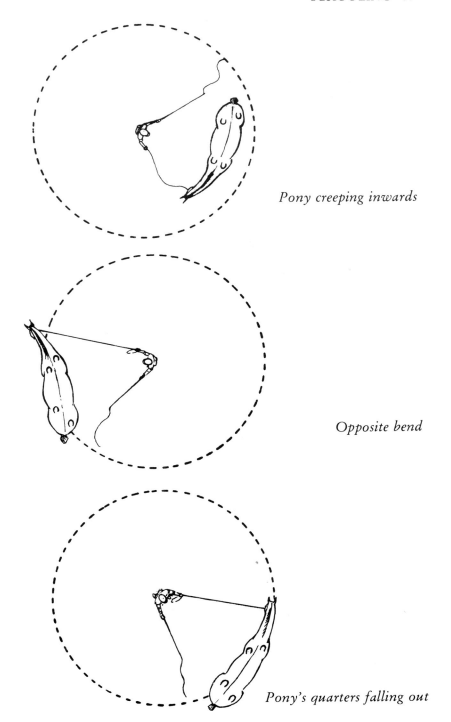

Pony creeping inwards

Opposite bend

Pony's quarters falling out

Side reins too loose

Side reins too tight

Side reins correctly adjusted

Bad outline on lunge

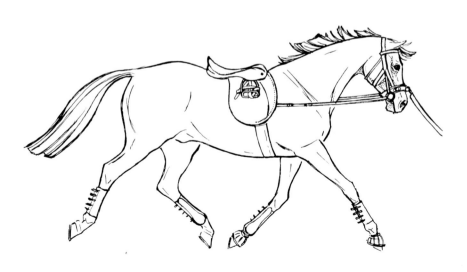

Good outline on lunge

especially with an older pony, all this will take time. Take care not to overwork the pony on his bad side. If you do, you will cause strain and stiffness and to avoid discomfort the pony will be forced to carry himself even more badly than ever. Correct bends are terribly important in the show-ring because all of the work is done on the circle and individual shows invariably include a figure of eight. Basic faults like this are best corrected on the lunge rather than under saddle.

Start your lungeing lessons with no more than ten minutes' slow work on each rein. Let your pony know that it *is* work and do not encourage him to buck and play about. If he has been properly fed and allowed some freedom in the paddock, he should not be encouraged to look upon his schooling sessions as a time to display high spirits, otherwise he may do it in the ring. Work at the walk and trot to begin with and do not introduce the canter until the pony is totally calm, obedient and balanced at the trot. Give your vocal commands clearly and firmly and always praise the pony for work well done. Establishing and maintaining a high standard of discipline does not mean you cannot be friendly and affectionate to your pony; rather, the reverse is true. The better your relationship and understanding, the better the result, because the pony will do his best to please you.

Never allow the pony to change the rein himself when he happens to feel like it. Ask for a halt, walk up to the pony (do not allow him to come to you) and turn him round yourself. Always remember that the cavesson is acting on the sensitive part of the nose. It should never be yanked or used roughly as this will cause injury and actually prevent the pony from going freely forward. Do not wrap the lunge rein around your hand, otherwise, if you are lungeing a strong pony and something frightens it, you could find yourself being dragged across the field. Hold the spare rein in loops, ready to be released immediately if necessary. Never let the line sag or touch the ground. As you become more experienced at lungeing, you can teach your pony to shorten and lengthen his stride and generally improve his gait. I cannot stress enough though that correct lungeing is an art. Properly done it is extremely beneficial, badly done it is useless and damaging.

There is no great mystery about schooling the show pony under saddle as good basic schooling is universal. There are many excellent books on the subject (see Recommended Reading at the end of the book) and it is impossible to go into it here in the

Walking towards the pony at halt

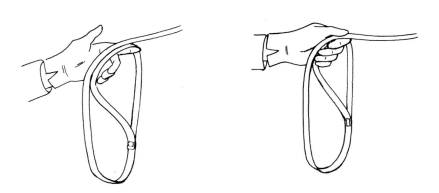

Coiling the lunge line

depth necessary to be helpful. I would advise anyone with a novice or unschooled animal to put themselves into the hands of one of our very talented producers for a week or two in order to set off on the right track. To get the best value for money you do need to go to a specialist, not a general riding school. Not all instructors, even highly qualified ones, have ring experience and understand your particular problems. It is difficult, impossible almost, to learn about schooling from a book, but I will try to set out some guidelines which may help.

A lot is written and even more is talked about head-carriage and most of it is nonsense. One thing is certain and that is that head-carriage and self-carriage cannot be satisfactorily obtained by artificial means. If you try to impose a correct head position on a pony by standing it in the stable for hours on end, trussed up with tight reins, over, and underchecks, and goodness knows what else as a substitute for proper training, the only result it can have is incorrect flexion, pain, stiffness and a hollow back, resulting in poor action, a dead mouth, and probably a ruined temperament into the bargain. Such an animal will be incapable of free, forward movement and, apart from that, such methods are extremely dubious and regarded by most producers with dismay.

There is no short cut to the well-schooled animal, whatever his purpose. Thorough basic training ensures that a pony slowly and systematically develops his ability and his muscles until he is able to carry himself and his rider correctly and confidently in a relaxed and happy manner without any artificial aid or support. If a pony's conformation does not allow it to achieve perfect carriage then one has to be satisfied with what it can achieve within its limitations and not seek to impose it artificially, which is not only foolish but cruel.

Ideal carriage is achieved when the pony is seen to be proceeding lightly and fluently, with rhythmic, regular steps, plenty of impulsion, with the front legs reaching forward from the shoulders and the hocks well engaged underneath. He will be 'on the bit', which means that the rider has a light and steady contact with the mouth, the jaw is relaxed and the poll flexed. The nose should be almost vertical to the ground and the overall effect is pleasing and very beautiful. Not many ponies achieve this perfection even in the show-ring, either through lack of expert schooling or limitations of a more physical kind. But do not let this put you off because a lot can be done at home to improve a pony's natural paces and made the very best of what he has.

All basic training should be done in a simple snaffle bridle and I would not advise the use of any martingales, running, or balancing reins at all, because for every problem you appear to solve by artificial means, you will surely create two more. If you are producing a novice pony, you will find that he must be exhibited in a simple snaffle bridle in novice classes and this is all very right and proper because a pony should not be ridden in a double bridle until he is going correctly and confidently in a snaffle.

Many people seem to think that a double bridle is the magic answer to head-carriage, balancing and control problems, but this is simply not the case. To put a pony into a double bridle too soon is madness. If he has not completely accepted the single bit, he will be horrified to find two in his mouth and a chain under his chin. Before you know where you are you will have a pony who is permanently behind the bit and skilled at every kind of evasion. Not only that, but you will lose free forward movement, resulting in ruined action and a ruined mouth. Never be tempted to rush this delicate transition and always bear in mind that the double bridle must be regarded as the icing on the cake, added not in order to disguise shortcomings, but to enhance the finished product.

The following comments are addressed to the person – jockey, groom, or producer – who is schooling the pony for the show-ring.

Of all the gaits the walk is surely the most difficult to improve. Being the slowest gait, it is hard to maintain impulsion, and a good active walk is a desirable natural asset. In the ring the pony should not slouch along, but neither should he give the impression of being hurried. If you are not sure what an active walk feels like, ride your pony down a gentle hill and this will give you an idea. He will, of necessity, reach well forward with his front legs, using his shoulders, and his hocks will come well under his body and feel very active. You will not necessarily be able to reproduce this as well on the flat, but it will give you something to work on. Encouraging the pony to walk out on the lunge properly will also help improve the gait.

When schooling at the walk, aim for a rhythmic, regular gait in which the pony covers a lot of ground. Never bustle along as this only shortens the stride, and guard against over-collection which will chop the stride and shorten the pony's front. It often helps to count the strides to assist in keeping a fluent, regular gait, especially through turns and circles when the pony tends either to slow or speed up. Half-halts will help to keep your pony's attention, they also aid balance and bring his hocks under. Always remember that all halts should be forward so push him into a resisting hand with your legs, never pull him back into a halt. Improvement will be a gradual process, but you will be helped in the ring by unfamiliar surroundings guaranteed to make any pony step out better, at least for the first few circuits!

At the trot, a good working pace is preferable to a flat out attempt to produce a semblance of extravagant action, which will probably only result in trailing hocks and an exaggeration of any tendency to lift the knee or throw out a leg. One sees children asking their ponies to fly along in the ring, displaying all their faults, either with their heads up in the air or, alternatively, going right into the ground. They would be so much better to slow down to a balanced, regular gait. A pony that really gets its toe out (extravagant action) will lap others quite naturally because it is using a much longer stride, but it is silly to bustle a pony along in an attempt to keep up, thus hiding any natural merit it might have.

Careful, steady schooling can do much to improve a scrappy, unbalanced trot. Again, work on the lunge will help, as will ridden work, preferably in a marked area with a good, level surface. Circles, half-halts, work on both reins, stride-counting to maintain a steady rhythmic pace, keeping the pony straight when you are working straight ahead and making sure that he is bending correctly when you are on a circle – all this will improve the gait. Work over poles on the ground set for trotting will help to balance a pony at the trot because he will have to look down, thus attaining a rounded top line, and he will have to use his hocks. It also adds variety to the schooling session. Trotting poles should be set out about 4-4½ft (1.2-1.3m) apart (less for a very tiny pony).

The canter should appear smooth and elegant. It can look rather stiff and 'rocking-horsy' if it is very slow, so it must be a steady but flowing gait. Some ponies have more comfortable canters than others and the way the rider sits can make all the

Working over trotting poles

difference. If he can absorb the movement with a relaxed seat and back, the effect is much more pleasing than that of the rider bumping up and down and being given a rough ride. Again, work on the lunge and schooling for a steady rhythmic pace, using circles, half-halts and work on both reins, will aid balance at the canter. During your road work remember that work up and down inclines is a good way to improve general tone, muscle and fitness, and the more developed your pony becomes, the easier it will be for him to use himself properly and give you good gaits.

It is very important that ponies, as well as their jockeys, are taught to gallop. It should never be allowed just to 'happen'. The gallop should be long and low, covering a lot of ground, and there should be no scuttling effect at all. Practise letting the pony out for a certain number of strides, perhaps ten to begin with, and then ease up at once. If you teach your pony to gallop in short bursts he will soon get the idea and he will be ready and waiting for the feel on the rein which tells him to come back to a canter. I think you must allow even the small ponies to flatten and really extend and you will be surprised how quickly they learn what is expected of them and how after the prescribed number of strides, they will often slow up on their own. Using the voice is often very helpful. I think it is very important for the ridden pony to show that he can and will really gallop (excluding the tinies of course), and also that he knows when and how to stop. Some ponies give only a few strides of a rather collected fast canter which is not enough because one immediately suspects that they cannot do more or that if they do they will buck or take off. At the other extreme there are those who lap the ring at a flat out pace for far too long and reduce the ringside to pale and trembling spectators. This is not good showmanship either! About ten strides of a low, long, controlled gallop down the long side of the ring is enough.

During the individual show most ponies are expected to canter a figure of eight with a simple change of leg, and the larger ponies are often asked to rein back.

To teach a pony (or a jockey) to ride a figure of eight, you can first mark out a very large one and trot the loops until they get the idea. After that you can canter the first loop, coming back to trot for a few strides before changing the leg and the bend for the second loop. If you stride count all the way round, this will maintain the pace and the rhythm and it will also help counteract rushing and anticipation on the part of the pony. When everything is going smoothly you can decrease the trot strides in the middle to the minimum, take away the markers and decrease the size of the figure of eight. After a while most show ponies can do their figure of eights without much prompting from the jockey at all.

To teach a pony to rein back you need a rider on the top and an assistant on the ground. The rider should use his legs to push the pony into a resisting hand, rather as if he was asking for a halt. The assistant should prevent the pony from moving forward by tapping the pony on the chest and at the same time he should say 'Back' firmly. The pony may be confused at first but he will soon get the idea and when he takes one step backwards, the rider should ask him to take a step forwards immediately afterwards before praising him. Be satisfied with one step at a time at first and always follow the step backwards with the same number of steps forward because this will keep the pony on the bit. The rider should keep the quarters straight by using his legs and the pony should step back calmly, moving his feet in pairs in a straight line, walking forward at once the same number of steps and the whole exercise should be performed in rhythm. The pony should not raise its head, drop the bit and run backwards with its quarters sticking out, yet this is often seen, even in the show-ring. Patience will eventually produce a good result. Forcing a pony back by pushing, or pulling him back with the reins will do no good at all. He just needs time to understand what is required of him.

When practising the individual display, do make sure that your transitions are smooth and unhurried. There should be no flapping about on the part of the rider and the pony should maintain a perfectly steady head-carriage throughout. Some ponies are not very quick to obey the rider's aids and nothing looks worse than a lot of obvious leg work going on. If the pony ignores the first aid, reinforce the next with a sharp tap with the whip behind the girth. Do this every time and it is in the pony's interest that you make sure that he feels it! After a while he will anticipate the tap and obey the first leg aid straightaway. Transitions down are probably more difficult and you should remember that all downward transitions are still forward movements. The pony should be pushed forward with the legs and seat into a resisting hand. He should never be allowed to flop into a lower place, neither should the rider pull with the reins and forget the legs. When this happens up comes the head and down go the quarters and it looks terrible.

Anticipation on the part of the pony can be a problem because an intelligent animal will soon get to know exactly what is expected of him and try to do it on his own before the rider has had a chance to ask. Guard against this by not practising too often, and by varying the show whenever you do. A schooled pony only needs to be run through his show once a week, possibly the day before the event. Any more than this will only lead to over-anticipation or boredom.

Too much schooling can make a pony stale. Fifteen minutes to start with, working up to half an hour, is plenty. Schooling should be followed by a ride so that pony and rider can enjoy themselves. Should a pony need more schooling, two half-hour sessions, morning and afternoon, are preferable to one long boring one and do try to vary the work. A thoughtful owner will be rewarded by a pony who enjoys his showing and that enjoyment is a tremendous asset in the ring.

Do not neglect to prepare your in-hand display. The first thing to do is to teach your pony to stand properly. Lead him along at a walk and ask him to halt. Carry a small stick and use it to tap the offending leg into place if he leaves one behind. A show pony should not stand like a hackney with all four legs stretched out, front and back. He should stand showing all four legs and the pair nearest to the judge should be the furthest apart. Such a position makes the pony appear to cover plenty of ground and improves his front.

If you take care to teach your pony to stand up properly, it will become a habit and your jockey will not have to push him about in an embarrassing manner in front of the judge. When you stand the pony out for inspection, you do not want him to stick his head in the air and stare about, neither do you want him to go to sleep. To make him lower his head, put his ears forward and stretch out his neck, thus making the most of his front, have some nuts in your pocket and use them to make him pay attention to you. Great care must be taken that the pony is never allowed to step forward. In the ring your jockey should be able to put his hand to his pocket and the pony should respond by pricking his ears and stretching out his neck towards him. You do not really want your jockey to have to pull grass or click his fingers in an obvious manner when the eyes of the world are upon them.

When you are showing your pony stripped (with the saddle off), it is most important that he leads well, level with your shoulder and carrying himself, not crowding you or hanging back. If he lags behind get an assistant to flip him from behind. After the first few times he will get to know what is wanted. To keep him walking away from you (leading-rein ponies should walk with a good length of rein between them and the attendant), use a stick to tap him away at the shoulder. All this is only a matter of patience in getting the pony used to doing it properly so that he carries on doing it out of habit. A pony who tows the leader along is a pain and this is often more difficult to correct. Look first at the feeding because if a pony is too pushy in hand he is probably too pushy in other ways. The fault could be in the diet or a matter of basic discipline. Lots of patience and in-hand work is the answer. Leading from a cavesson will give you extra control, as will side-reins. Really, if you have this problem it is back to the basic road work discussed in the previous chapter.

If you have done your work on the lunge thoroughly, your pony should walk, trot, halt and stand readily to command which is a great asset when you are leading the pony up for the judge's individual appraisal. You will be expected to stand the pony up properly for his inspection, walk the pony away and turn and trot back and past him so that he can see the pony move from the front and the back. Be quite merciless at home in getting a good walk and not a crawl. Turn the pony away from you (you go the long way round) and give the commend to trot at once so that the pony goes forward off his hocks. The last thing you want is to have to drag the pony into a trot otherwise out will go the neck, back will go the ears and the hocks will trail along behind.

If your pony's action is less than perfect, a sedate trot will minimise his faults; you can only speed up if you have nothing to hide and there is no point in flying along, so that everyone marvels at your speed and action and forgets to look at the pony! It is also important to lead the pony absolutely straight, not on a wobble. Most judges prefer a steady, straight balanced run up to a spectacular flash past which does not give them time to see anything.

As part and parcel of this in hand training, you should teach your pony to stand still for quite long periods of time without fidgeting about and get him used to having hands run down his legs, his neck felt, his feet and tail lifted and even his teeth looked at. All this is soon accomplished at home if it is carried out as part of his routine but it can be an upsetting experience in the ring if a pony is not schooled for it. You must also get your pony used to having rosettes (the bigger the better) hooked onto his bridle and you can even stage mock presentations with silver cups and trays. This may seem a bit extreme but it is amazing how many ponies take fright at prize-giving and it seems a shame if your jockey has ridden the pony into the winners against all odss and is denied the pleasure of the reward because the pony is unprepared!

All the previous advice is, of course, relevant to the working hunter pony, who has to show his paces on the flat as well as over fences. The basic conditioning and schooling, the flat work, and the requirements of the individual show and in-hand display are the same, the only difference is in the type of pony being shown.

It has been true in the past and will certainly be true in the future that many a fine working hunter pony will fail because the basic training has been neglected. Performance alone is not enough because an unschooled pony is an unsuitable mount for a child, especially in the hunting field, where he will be a danger to everyone. I stress that you must be meticulous about your basic training. You must get your flat work absolutely right before you begin to do any serious schooling for jumping.

Schooling the working hunter pony for jumping is a rather different matter from schooling a pony for show-jumping. The methods must differ since you must set out to develop initiative, boldness and self-sufficiency over fences. The ideal hunting pony is clever and brave. He can look after himself and his jockey, take off where he can and get over as best he might. There is not time to gauge take-offs out hunting, and if you try to count strides and place your pony by 'hooking-back' in the working hunter pony ring, you will be penalised.

Helping a novice pony to gain courage and start to enjoy his jumping is very rewarding. You can begin by looking for small, straightforward obstacles to hop over during your rides. Logs and ditches are ideal. If you are an adult, your neck is your own responsibility, but if your jockey rides out alone you should take care that he does not jump alone, especially on an inexperienced pony. Accidents do happen and a child could lie injured, miles from anywhere or anyone. Also you must make sure that your ponies do not trespass on growing crops and farmland and if you build fences on bridleways, remove them afterwards because the next person may be a beginner, or even a cyclist!

As a general rule, when bringing on a novice pony you should give him plenty of encouragement with your legs and voice but leave his mouth alone, apart from keeping him straight. Let him find his own way over and be sure to praise him when he does. If he gets excited and starts to fuss or rush at the obstacles, be very careful to stay absolutely calm yourself and never let the situation develop into an angry tug-of-war. If you make small obstacles part of every ride, pretty soon it will become routine and not a madly exciting event.

As the pony gains confidence, you can build some small natural fences at home. Bear in mind that to school over flimsy fences is useless because as soon as an intelligent pony learns that he can knock them down, he will become careless. Later, when he

Helping a novice pony to gain courage and start to enjoy his jumping is very rewarding

meets the real thing in the ring he will come a cropper and lose his courage.

There is an abundance of suitable material to construct natural fences from at very little cost – logs, troughs, coops, planks and rustic poles. Even old doors will do provided you remove any sharp protruberances. Bunches of brush or twigs tied with baler twine, bales and old tyres make good fillers and you can dig open ditches, although if you rent your land you may have to seek permission first. Whatever you use keep it low to start with and make it look substantial. Construct all kinds of different obstacles and when the pony is jumping single low fences happily, construct a course. Personally I feel it is a good idea to introduce your pony to coloured poles because although you should not encounter them in the working hunter pony classes, you probably will. You will certainly meet a painted wall sooner or later, not to mention coloured fertiliser bags!

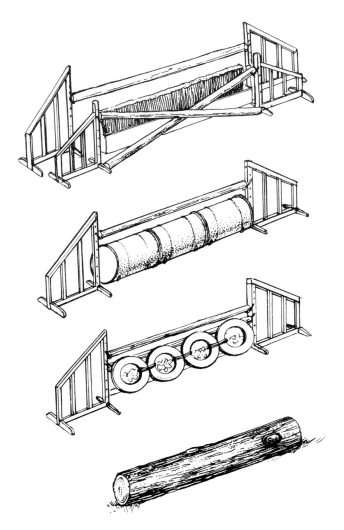

Jumps for the working hunter pony

A BSPS course will contain not fewer than five obstacles. There will be spreads as well as uprights and probably a combination fence and an in-and-out. There may even be a gate to open and a water-jump. Because the course is designed to be ridden at a good hunting pace (a strong canter), there will not be any tight turns but some fences will be angled and there will be a change of direction. It will be seen then, that the pony must be ridden intelligently round. The jockey must have absolute control and although he should not show-jump the pony round the course, he should be able to shorten and lengthen the stride to deal with the combinations, spreads and uprights. Those jockeys who can only steer round the course and gallop at the fences will be in trouble, as will the jockey who tries to show-jump every fence and ends up in a muddle over a line of related fences designed for the longer, faster pace.

As a rough guide to the construction of schooling fences the distances between are not less than 60ft (18m), and the distance inside the pen is not less than 22ft (6.7m). The recommended distances for spreads are

Intermediate W.H.	3ft 3in–4ft 3in spread (97.5–127.5cm)
15hh class	3ft 3in–4ft 3in spread (97.5–127.5cm)
14hh class	2ft 9in–3ft 9in spread (82.5–112.5cm)
13hh class	2ft 3in–3ft 3in spread (67.5–97.5cm)
Nursery	1ft 9in–2ft 9in spread (52.5–82.5cm)
Cradle	1ft 6in–2ft 6in spread (45–75cm)

The recommended heights for fences are

Intermediate W.H.	Min. 3ft–Max. 3ft 9in (90–112.5cm)
15hh class	Min. 3ft–Max. 3ft 9in (90–112.5cm)
14hh class	Min. 2ft 9in–Max. 3ft 3in (82.5–97.5cm)
13hh class	Min. 2ft 6in–Max. 3ft (75–90cm)
Nursery	Min. 2ft–Max. 2ft 6in (60-75cm)
Cradle	Min. 1ft 9in–Max. 2ft 3in (52.5–67.5cm)

Width for water

Intermediate W.H.	10ft (3m)
15hh class	10ft (3m)
14hh class	8ft (2.4m)
13hh class	6ft (1.8m)

There is not enough room here to go into jumping technique and schooling problems, but there is some recommended reading at the end of the book which may be helpful. If you are lucky enough to be able to take your pony and jockey to a good instructor who also has a cross-country course, then do take full advantage of it. Hunter trials are also ideal training for the working hunter pony, and if you can take him hunting so much the better. After all, it is what the class is all about.

When schooling the more experienced child and pony over

larger obstacles, for safety's sake they should knock down if they are hit very hard, they should still look solid. Take care not to overface the pony by asking for too much too soon. Boldness and courage are terribly precious attributes and they are gained bit by bit, by happy experience. It is the same with the jockey. If the pony gets into a muddle over a fence, do not make him tackle it again straightaway. Rebuild his confidence first by jumping some easier fences before you go back to the bogey. Guard against making your working pony too precious; he should not be over-protected. It is silly to keep pony and jockey from going hunting or to pony club events and hunter trials when it is so vitally important that they have an enjoyable partnership and the mutual trust that these things help build. The odd scrape and blemish will not count against the pony in the ring because the judges are aware that these are, after all, working ponies. By that, I do not mean that a pony can be patterned all over his legs with splints, curbs, thoroughpins, windgalls, and the like. Fair wear and tear is one thing but unsightly limbs are quite another!

The height and age classification for working ponies is as follows:

Pony exceeding 14hh but not exceeding 15hh. Rider not over 18 years

Pony exceeding 13hh but not exceeding 14hh. Rider not over 16 years.

Pony not exceeding 13hh. Rider not over 14 years.

Nursery stakes. Pony not exceeding 13hh. Rider not over 12 years

Cradle stakes. Pony not exceeding 12hh. Rider not over 10 years.

Intermediate classes are for ponies exceeding 14.2hh and not exceeding 15.2hh. Riders between the ages of 16 and 25 years.

In novice classes the minimum becomes the maximum height and spread.

(No water jumps, other than as hazards in Nursery or Cradle Stakes.)

Apart from in the Novice classes, ponies must be four years old or over and any horse or pony who has won £300 in prize money under BSJA or any other National Federation rules here or overseas is ineligible to compete. No jockey may ride more than one pony in any class and there may be no change of rider from Phase 1 to Phase 2. Ponies and riders are allowed to compete in both Cradle and Nursery Stakes at the same show, but in no other WHP class. Riders in the Nursery Stakes may compete in the open, WHP classes at the same show. Ponies in the Nursery Stakes only are not eligible to compete in the open 13 hands class. In mixed height classes, competitors must still compete in their correct height section and be the correct age for the height of pony they are riding.

CHAPTER SEVEN

Show Pony Jockey

Restricted Open and Novice

Show-ring riders are not generally renowned for their riding ability and this is largely a legacy of the past, when riders sat as far back in the saddle as they possibly could, stuck their feet forward as a safety precaution, and let their reins lie in festoons to display (or suggest) a good front. Even so, a great number of our present-day riders who have achieved fame, if not fortune, in other spheres started off in the show-ring: Ted Edgar, Jenny Loriston-Clark, David Broome and Eddie Macken for instance, to name but a few.

Yet there are still some fearful sights to be seen in the ridden pony classes, and there really is no excuse to be made for it. The 'Water Skiing' position is still the biggest horror of the show-ring, closely followed by the 'Quasimodo' (shoulders hunched, hands clenched in the stomach) position, not to mention the wobbly, flapping legs, stuck out elbows and toes and all the other awful things that go on aboard the most lovely ponies. I cannot advise any producer enough to have their jockey properly taught by a really good instructor. You do not have to go to a specialist to learn basic equitation after all, so it need not cost the earth.

This is not a book to tell you how to teach your jockey to ride, so I am not going to go into seats and things but I will stress that a well-trained jockey is as important as a well-trained pony. A skilled jockey can bring a less well-trained pony several places up the line, but a poor rider on the best pony in the class can keep it out of the prizes. Also, although the best person to school a show pony is often an experienced, lightweight adult, a good jockey can lighten the load considerably and obviously the more time the jockey and the pony spend together the better the relation-ship, which can only be beneficial for all concerned. If there are any problems between pony and rider, take a deep breath, dig deep into your pockets and send them both for a crash course with a top producer. This will repay you dividends.

The amount of time your jockey has available for riding will depend on outside influences, school being the prime factor.

Many jockeys, especially borrowed ones, only have a short schooling session the evening before the show, and this may be all a well-schooled pony and an experienced jockey need. You may be lucky enough to be able to school your pony and your jockey together throughout your conditioning and schooling programme. Whichever way you do it, it is a mistake to regard your jockey as little more than a decoration. He is half of the partnership and, as such, can make or break it.

Immaculate turnout of pony and rider is a matter of close attention to detail and as the standard is so terribly high and level these days, classes are often won or lost on it. I make no apology for going into even the minor points of presentation.

To begin with: the jockeys. Hats, even if they are not new, should be well brushed or wiped with a damp cloth to remove dust. Steaming over a kettle spout will bring up any flattened pile. Hats should be worn straight, not tipped up at the front with the peak pointing heavenwards. The tinies are rather soft in the head (this is a biological fact, not an insult) and they should wear elastic under the chin to keep the hat on. Older children who aspire to elegance should have hats that really fit, so they do not need it. Unfortunately hats that really fit are usually ones that have been made to measure by the Very Best People, and the Best People are expensive. If the hat cannot be made to measure and does not stay put when you hold your jockey upside down by the ankles and give him a good shake (I'm joking) then you will have to sacrifice a little elegance for the sake of safety and put up with the elastic. Do not think you can disguise it, though, by using pink knicker elastic!

Hats come in a variety of shapes and there are also differences in the depth of the velvet pile. The shape of the hat must suit the jockey. A small child with a large head, for instance, given a high-pile, deep-crown hat, could look as if he was wearing a busby, so do try the alternatives before you decide. Some children look very nice in a bowler hat and this is perfectly correct to wear in the ring. The same rules apply. It must be well brushed, well fitting, and be worn absolutely straight. Safety harness is not generally used in the show-ring for aesthetic reasons except in the working hunter pony jumping phase, when a correctly secured skull cap must be worn, usually topped with a silk.

Of course a nice hat is no good at all if the hair underneath looks awful. Boys are lucky because their hair is worn fairly short

A nice hat is no good at all if the hair underneath looks awful. A severely disciplined style is essential.
(Photos: Dr Gilbert Scott)

anyway and it is fairly easy to keep looking neat. Girls have more complex problems. A short hairstyle still needs a net to prevent any spiky bits from sticking out and no hair should be visible on the forehead. The only forelock should be between the pony's ears! Short hair, though, does not suit everyone, so a slightly longer style which looks attractive with a riding hat is a rolled-under pageboy cut, netted to stay in place. Otherwise you could try flicking the hair up and out round the sides of the hat, however, I am assured that this style needs hair with body and a jockey with sufficient dedication to sleep in pins the night before! It is not a style for the faint hearted because it cannot be netted, so if your jockey has not got the right kind of hair, forget it. It looks frightful if the curl starts to drop out.

Hair any longer than will roll under neatly can go into bunches. Freshly washed hair in small bunches tied with neat ribbons can look very attractive. The ribbon should be a dark colour and not too wide. Navy or navy-spotted ribbons are popular, or you can match your ribbons to the colour of tie, buttonhole and the pony's browband if you want to be very chic. Long bunches tied with pink satin ribbons and similar Alice-in-Wonderland effects are in bad taste!

Once the hair gets past the bunches stage, it looks best in a low-slung pony tail. A short one can still be netted to achieve a neat outline. Plaits are better than an untidy, long pony tail. One plait or two looks very neat. Some riders loop up the plaits and this looks very nice. Elastic bands will help them stay put.

Buns are very elegant but they are tricky things and need as much practice as a figure of eight. They have to be fairly low in the neck because of the hat and they must be securely pinned and netted, especially if the hair is newly washed and slippery. If the bun starts to come out during the individual show, everyone will ignore your pony's beautiful gallop and rein-back and stare in horrified fascination at the back of your jockey's neck.

Shirts should always be well fitting at the collar which means that a female jockey cannot borrow one from her father. The points should lie flat, not turn up like a forgotten sandwich. Your jockey needs plenty of room in the shoulders for free move-ment. White is the obvious choice for a shirt, but it is permissible to be a little more adventurous in the working hunter pony rings. You might try a navy and white check for instance, with a navy coat and a plain navy tie, or a toning plain colour with a tweed

Jane Hankey wears a tweed jacket with a velvet collar. Cawdor Helen,
W.H.P. Champion, literally covered with glory

jacket. As a general guide, if you would not wear it in the hunting field, it is not correct in the working pony rings either. Plain or discreetly patterned ties are recommended and even a Pony Club tie is not really smart enough for the ridden pony classes.

No buttonhole is usual in the working hunter pony classes, only a neat badge. In the ridden show pony classes, most people sport some kind of decoration. Never be persuaded that your jockey should sport half a bridal bouquet. A full-blown rose garnished with maiden-hair fern might be acceptable at a wedding, but it will not charm the judge at Windsor. A tiny bud or a single bloom no larger than a two pence piece is correct. To save trouble you can sew a neat artificial flower to the lapel but it must look fresh and life-like and it must not be plastic! Match the flower to your accessories if possible, as this helps to make an attractive overall picture.

These days you can buy all kinds of jackets suitable for the show-ring – navy, green, brown, plum, grey, or check, all beautifully cut with smart velvet collars to match the hat. The choice of colour is yours alone but bear in mind that the coat and hat must go together. A wine-coloured coat will be absolutely ruined if you choose to team it with a hat in spring-cabbage green. In the working hunter pony classes you have rather less choice. You are, after all, wearing hunt dress, so a plum or green coat will not do at all. Navy, black or tweed are safe bets. To be strictly correct you should also sew up the ribbons on the back of your hat (only hunt servants are supposed to have them hanging down), but this is a fine point and not many people pay attention to it.

Showing coats are very expensive and one of the prime considerations in selecting one for your jockey is that it should really *fit*. Never buy a showing coat two sizes too big so that your jockey can 'grow into it'. Most saddlers and riding outfitters have a stock of good second-hand jackets and it is far better and cheaper to keep swopping coats than to risk your jockey looking like Little Orphan Annie. Beware of buying a coat too small because it looks a perfect fit in the shop. Sit your jockey on a chair and make sure the coat is not too short. If it is, it will hang above the saddle and make your pony appear to have a long back. Sleeves go up a little bit with wear so look for a little extra length in the shop. If the coat is too short in the arms, the gap between the glove and the sleeve will spoil the appearance. New or second-hand, care for the coat well. Have it cleaned regularly, keep it brushed and on a well-shaped wooden hanger, not a throw-away wire one which will ruin the line of the shoulders. Do not allow your jockey to make the pockets bulge with his belongings and be sure to insist on a change of clothing as soon as he comes out of the ring.

Everybody wears stretch jodhpurs these days, they fit all shapes, and wash beautifully and look very smart. If they tend to ride up and show your jockey's socks, turn down the turnup and add some broad foot elastic in black or brown to match the boots. Foot elastic is worn by even the smartest people. Watch that your jockey wears short socks not three-quarter length ones held up by elastic which causes an unsightly ridge half way up the calf. Riding clothiers sell jodhpurs in the most amazing colours but tradition dies hard in the show-ring and you should stick to

Excellent turnout. Neat hair, taped number, leather-covered cane, foot elastic. The jacket sleeves are too short leaving an awkward gap. The pony is Perry Ditch March Winds, a 14.2hh champion with marvellous pony character

Well fitting jacket and stretch jodhpurs. Carroll Cooper on Centurion Minuet

beige, white, lemon, or cream shades. As a general rule, white and beige go with grey and chestnut ponies, lemon or cream with the bays. Keep your jodhpurs spotlessly clean and if you get a pulled thread do not cut it off otherwise you will make a hole. Pull the thread through to the other side and keep your jockey away from brambles!

Jodhpur boots can be brown or black; elastic sides are neater than strap sides. Long riding boots are not worn in the ridden pony classes except in the 15 hand class, but they are often seen in the working hunter pony rings in the 14 hands and 15 hands classes. This is because they are invaluable when your jockey is leading the pony through a ford, diving through a bullfinch, or getting his leg trapped in the swinging gate! Long boots are only elegant when they fit. They should fit as snugly as possible and come as far up to the knee as will still allow free movement. Calf-length boots look terrible. The straps should buckle at the front with the ends facing outwards. Personally, I dislike rubber boots for the show-ring and if you cannot afford leather, I think you should stick to good jodhs and jodhpur boots. Not everyone will agree though.

Show secretaries imagine you need at least twenty yards of white string to fix your jockey's number on, either that or they give you a piece four inches too short. Provide yourself with measured lengths of coloured tape to match your jacket. You can get it from any haberdashery counter. On the subject of gloves, go for brown or black leather. They will be freezing in the cold and slippery in the rain, but it will not hurt your jockey to learn early that one must suffer a little to achieve true elegance! Traditional white or yellow string gloves are too glaring and they draw attention to the hands which is unfortunate if they are not as steady as they could be.

A leather-covered cane completes the outfit for ridden pony classes. Never use any kind of whip with loops or fiddly smackers on the end. If you cannot rise to a leather-covered cane, a bamboo one will do just as well. You can use a hunting-whip in the working hunter pony classes or, because it is still a show class, use a cane if you prefer. Long schooling-whips should never be taken into the ring and the riders of leading-rein ponies do not carry a stick at all, although it is perfectly correct for their handlers to do so. I must admit that the only time I ever used mine was to poke my pony awake during the interminable judging sessions. Back protectors may be worn in the jumping phase of the working hunter pony classes.

Speaking of leading-rein ponies, a word about dress for their attendants. It is very easy for a man to look smart in the ring because the choice of clothing is so limited anyway. A dark suit, echoing the colour of the jockey's coat is ideal. The male handler should wear a hat. A bowler is professional but it is possible to wear something a little more casual and still look the part.

As far as ladies are concerned, one does see some sights! It is throwing away valuable first impressions of overall appearance to go into the ring with a nice pony wearing a scruffy anorak and wellington boots, yet many do. By the same rule, to wear high heels, fancy stockings, a frivolous dress and an Ascot hat is just as bad because nobody will be looking at the pony! Ladies should wear a plain, smart suit, skirt or trousers, it really does not matter. Generally the darker the colour, the more professional it will look. The smarter shows will not allow you into the ring without suitable headgear, so keep a felt hat or a horsy headscarf handy always, even if you prefer to show without. Be sure to wear sensible shoes because you have to run with the pony and the show-ring turf is by no means bowling-green standard. The attendant can wear riding clothes and some prefer to do so, matching their outfit as near as possible to that of the jockey to help make an attractive picture. Whatever the attendant chooses to wear, he must be well turned out as a compliment to the show, the pony and the judge.

Lots of the points in this chapter are equally applicable to children competing in turn-out, pairs and side-saddle classes. For the latter, if you can have a habit made to measure, so much the better, because some of the habits that drape the jockeys often look as if they once belonged to great-grandma, and have not been altered either! The trouble with old fashioned habits is that they have impossibly tight sleeves and are too full in the skirt. The modern side-saddle apron is a neat and narrow affair. It does not fly in the breeze and make the jockey look like an extra in *Dick Turpin*. Take care, though, that the apron is not cut too short, showing acres of inelegant boot and advertising the colour of the breeches above the saddle.

Children look over-dressed in silk hats and veils. They look far more natural in velvet caps; or if you prefer it is perfectly correct for your jockey to wear a bowler hat. Side-saddle classes are a joy to watch when the exhibits are beautifully turned out; often, though, there is someone in the class who looks merely comical – be sure the jockey is not yours!

CHAPTER EIGHT

Saddlery for the Show-Ring

Working Pony Classes

You can show a working hunter pony in any type of suitable bridle and, generally speaking, the plainer the better. Very thin 'bootlace' leatherwork does not flatter a plain head, and as one would not use it for hunting, neither is it suitable for working hunter pony classes. A thicker, more workmanlike bridle is best. Drop nosebands and running martingales are permitted, but you do occasionally come across a judge who considers that they are artificial aids and docks a point accordingly.

As you are not allowed to change any saddlery during the phases, the same tack will have to see you through the showing and the jumping. You may be perfectly happy on the flat with a simple snaffle bridle, but if your pony needs a stronger bit for the jumping then this is the one to use.

Bits and bitting are a complex subject and if you ask an equitation expert if you should use a more severe bit to give your jockey more control, you will probably get short shrift and be told that the answer lies not in a more severe bit but in more and better schooling. This may certainly be true in the case of a young pony whose basic training has been skimped, but the ideal working hunter pony is bold and brave, he is ridden by a child who, often as not, simply has not the experience or the strength to sit down and hold, he wants to get on with the job and the class is judged over solid fences and at speed.

Anyone who has shown working hunter ponies will know that, faced with a row of inviting rustic fences with plenty of grass between, some ponies who really love their jumping become over-enthusiastic, and any amount of schooling flies straight out of the window. It is never a joke to watch your child (or anyone else's, for that matter), struggling to prevent a pony galloping flat out over fixed fences, and it certainly gets the pair nowhere in the class because they are not able to cope with angled fences, combinations set for a steadier pace, and changes of direction.

If your pony has a good mouth, there is nothing to beat a simple hollow eggbut jointed snaffle and you can use a running

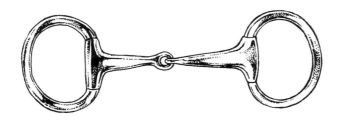

Hollow German eggbutt snaffle

martingale if it helps. There is a fashion for the drop noseband at present, but I honestly can't see that it does very much apart from discouraging a pony from opening his mouth and crossing his jaw. If your pony gets his head up and goes on too fast at his fences, you need a bit which will induce direct flexion and have a head-lowering effect to enable the jockey to stay in control. This means you must use either a double bridle or a pelham. Pelhams are very much disliked in some circles, but, nevertheless, many ponies go very well in them and, provided that you attach two reins, I would rather see a pony in a pelham, than in a double bridle, suffering a mouthful of bits that the child hasn't the experience to use correctly. In all things concerning children and ponies, common sense, even at the expense of equitation, must prevail, and the safety of the child must be the first priority.

It seems rather basic advice, I know, to say that you must be

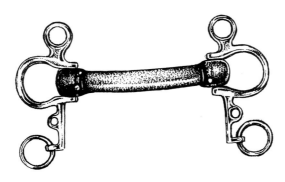

Pelham – correct with the addition of a curb chain and two reins, but can be used with a single rein and 'D' pieces

sure that the bit is the right size for the pony's mouth but a bit too small will pinch, and one too large will not act on the mouth properly and this can make all the difference to how the pony goes. Make sure also that the bridle fits correctly. A browband that is too small will irritate and cause head-shaking, a throat lash too tight will cause a pony to yaw. Over-large (or too small) cheek pieces will put the buckles in the wrong place, all of which will spoil the look of the pony's head. Do use a lip strap if the bit has rings for one as it will be incorrect without and it will also prevent the curb-chain from acting too high up.

A plain leather browband should be used; do not be tempted to use a coloured one. If your jockey finds plain leather reins slippery, plaited ones are a better bet than rubber-covered ones. I must admit that I always use rubber-covered reins for hunting but they are unsightly, do not wear well, and when they are new and get damp, gloves, breeches and horse's neck turn orange!

Saddles are an important consideration in working hunter pony classes. Nothing looks worse than a jockey trying to sit properly over fences on a showing saddle with cut back flaps. Find a comfortable general-purpose saddle which fits the pony and gives your jockey a comfortable ride. No one in his right mind would send a child out hunting on a showing saddle and it looks just as stupid in the ring. You may use a numnah if you

Working hunter pony tack

wish but make sure it is not too large for the saddle, or too small, and that it is the same shape. Take your saddle with you when you select one. A leather Balding or Atherstone girth is preferable to webbing or string.

Stainless steel is expensive, but it is the best metal for bits and stirrups and it will save you hours of polishing. Make sure that your stirrups are the right size for your jockey; if they are too small his feet will get stuck, hampering dismounting and running the risk of him being dragged if he fell. If they are too large, the foot could slip right through and the same thing could happen. Well-designed safety stirrups are ideal for tinies and many jockeys like rubber treads in their stirrups, essential if the bottom has worn smooth. No boots or bandages are allowed in the working pony ring, whips must be no longer than 30in (75cm), and spurs are forbidden.

Riding Pony Classes

Plain snaffle bridles are compulsory in first ridden, leading-rein and novice pony classes, double bridles are correct otherwise, although in classes for pairs and groups you can please yourself. The best leatherwork for the ridden pony classes is high quality leather: dark, supple, and thin enough to show off a pretty head to advantage. Again, stainless steel is best for bits, stirrups and buckles. In the ridden classes fancy browbands are almost always used, velvet, not plastic, usually in the producer's own colour or colours, echoed in the tie, buttonhole and ribbons (if any) of the

Bits for a double bridle

jockey. The noseband can be stitched or made of rolled leather. If you like the latter, you can have browband and reins made up to match, but the pony needs to have a lovely head to carry it off. Try several styles and widths of noseband on your pony if possible, adjusting them higher or lower until you find the one that suits him best.

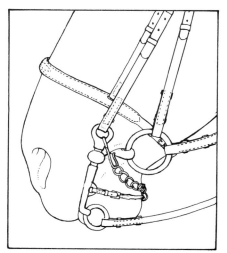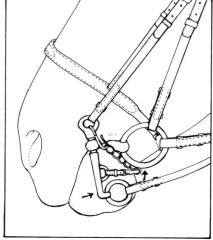

A correctly fitting curb chain acts on the chin when the cheek-piece is drawn back at an angle of 45 degrees

For leading-rein ponies, I favour a dark, narrow leather leading-rein rather than a tubular white one; then if you step on it just before you go into the ring it is not the end of the world! The whitener tends to come off the tubular ones, disastrous if you are wearing a dark suit. If you cannot find a leather one, a saddler will make you one quite reasonably, with a clip or buckle end. Do be sure to have it made long enough.

Saddles for the ridden show pony can make or mar the picture. Obviously the prime consideration is that they should really fit. Saddles on tiny ponies often sit up too high in front. This is because the tinies tend to be rather round. Your saddler will probably be able to fit a point strap (a girth strap in front of the normal ones), or re-arrange the stuffing to suit the pony. Certainly you must do something about it because the saddle will tilt your rider backwards onto the back of the saddle. You should still be able to see daylight from front to back though: on no account should the saddle rest on the wither or the spine.

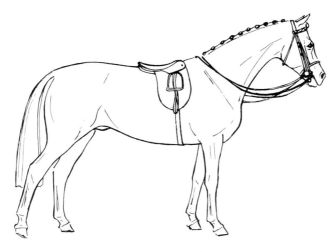

Show pony tack

A show saddle is cut straight to show off the shoulder and this effect is spoiled if the saddle tends to work forward. Again, a point strap can make all the difference and a strip of pimpled rubber sewn onto the centre underside of a tubular girth will help. If your pony has a good girth line and the saddle does not slip, use a narrow dark leather girth instead. It looks nicer and is easier to keep clean. Buy good quality stirrup leathers and in the case of tiny riders, if they are too long, trim them off or fold them and keep them in place with two elastic bands. Long flapping ends will spoil the picture.

When choosing a saddle for your pony, consider not only his size and shape, but also the size of the jockey. A tiny saddle on a pony that tends to be slightly long in the back will accentuate it, but do not go too far and swamp the animal so that your jockey rolls about like a pea on a drum. By the same ruling, if the pony is very compact, make sure that the saddle is not too large, giving the impression of having all the wheels underneath. Accommodate your jockey by all means but look at it from all points of view.

Obviously the combination will perform that much better if they are comfortable and some saddles intended for use on show ponies are abominable. The object of a show saddle is to give the animal a long frontage and a good top line. Therefore the flaps are cut straight, or even slightly back, and a skeleton tree is used to make the seat fairly straight and close to the back. A point strap is usually added to prevent the saddle shifting forward, and the bars are extended or set back so that the rider does not have to ride with the leg over the buckle of the stirrup leather. All this means that it is difficult for a child to sit naturally and correctly on a show saddle, and the shape of it does not actually encourage good riding. Some producers have tried dressage saddles for showing but generally the seats are too deep, thus breaking up the pony's top line and the rider tends to ride rather long (a disaster if the jockey is already tall), and there is often too much flap, not to mention the problem posed by extended girth straps, although these can be lopped off. It is easier, though, for a jockey to show off the paces of a pony riding on a dressage saddle and some saddlers are beginning to realise this and produce better show saddles with a slightly deeper seat and more leg room.

Side-saddles are less of a problem owing to the fact that they are being made today and it is obviously advisable to buy the most expensive saddle you can possibly afford and have it made especially for your pony and your jockey. I can imagine some long faces on receipt of this advice and I will add that if you are just trying the class to see how you like it, it is possible to get a second-hand saddle if you advertise in the horsy press and take great care that what you buy is a modern straight-seated (as opposed to a comfortable-looking bowl shape) saddle in good order that really fits the pony and jockey. I have in the past ridden a horse in a saddle too large and disappeared slowly down the side of the animal like the setting sun, and I can tell you it is a most unpleasant way to go! Naturally, if you are considering side-saddle classes, you will realise that your pony needs to have long, smooth paces, a good front and a well developed wither. It will not matter if he is slightly long in the back. It is also important to have your jockey instructed by an expert. The Ladies Side-Saddle Association will put you in touch with someone in your area.

Any new pieces of tack can be quickly toned in with the rest by an overnight soak in neat's foot oil. You cannot do this with saddles though, so if you need a new one, go for one in dark leather, or get a second-hand one which has already mellowed. A glaringly new orange saddle or bridle gives the novice away at once in the show ring.

Tack is always expensive. Showing tack is even more so. But if you buy top quality leather and metalwork it will last a lifetime and prove a good investment. It seems unnecessary to stress that something so costly must be really well looked after, cleaned regularly, hung up properly, and that it is unwise to use narrow leatherwork for schooling and exercise when ordinary tack will do the job better. Tack which is well cared for all of the time will not need any special attention before it is ready for use in the ring. A quick buffing up should be all that is necessary.

Show tack requires a rather different general cleaning technique to look really good. The trouble with tack cleaned with ordinary saddle soap, excellent though it is, is that it goes dull quickly and attracts dust. Likewise if you just use oil on your tack it goes almost black and rather flabby and a after a while it won't shine at all. The tried and tested way to deal with show tack is to clean the upper surface with the required shade of boot polish (dark tan to dark brown) to get a hard bright waterproof shine (you can even use water in the army spit and polish manner for added sparkle) and to soap the underside only to retain suppleness. Take care that you do not neglect the soaping or you will find that your precious leatherwork cracks up in a remarkably short time. I prefer to stick to the traditional saddle soap as far as the saddle is concerned for the comfort of the rider and the person who has to wash the jodhpurs! It does no harm though to buff up the pommel and the cantle now and again and to disguise any scratch marks with boot polish.

Stable Clothing

The basic necessities for a show pony in the stable are fairly simple. For a start he will need a good quality jute rug, preferably fully lined. Under this you will need at least two blankets. The traditional orange-striped ones are very warm but they are also alarmingly heavy for a small pony. I used to use hospital-type Lan-air-cel blankets on my tinies, finding them light, warm and easy to wash and quick to dry. Army blankets are usually good and cheap and fairly tough. Three will replace two traditional horse blankets.

Check them both over very carefully. Carola Williams on Solway Sweet William 1972

When your pony's coat is through and the weather gets warmer you will take off a layer or two and you might like to put a light-weight washable sheet on under the blanket and rug to keep out the dust. An old single-sized shortened bed sheet is ideal. Wash this under-sheet often. Most laundries will clean horse blankets. Have them washed, rather than dry-cleaned. Rug sizes are standard and the following guide may be useful to you if you are buying new ones or twirling needle and thread to adapt blankets and bed sheets!

A pony up to	11	hands needs a	3ft 9" rug	(113cm)
	12		4ft	(120cm)
	12.2		4ft 3"	(128cm)
	13		4ft 6"	(135cm)
	13.2		4ft 9"	(143cm)
	14		5ft	(150cm)
	14.2		5ft 3"	(158cm)
	15		5ft 6"	(165cm)

The above table may vary slightly if the pony is very compact or long in the back and to measure the animal you should place the tape at the middle of the breast and take it to where you would expect the back of the rug to be, along the side of the pony to the hind-quarters. Bear in mind that if you intend to put three blankets underneath, it will take the rug up at least 2in (5cm).

For day wear, if you like your pony to look smart to impress any rivals who may be snooping around weighing up the competition, a wool and mohair day rug is very nice, especially in your very own colours with your initials on it. An exercise sheet designed to wear during exercise, as used in racing stables, is also a good idea for cold weather work. They are put on under the saddle and need a fillet string to prevent them blowing up. It is possible to use a day rug instead but it will be rather more bulky and difficult to arrange under the saddle. A mackintosh or Gannex sheet may be used in wet weather.

A roller should be selected with care because, like the saddle, it must fit the pony. A padded one is essential for a pony who is wearing rugs all the time and it pays to buy the very best quality. Iron-arch rollers are anti-cast (they prevent the pony from rolling over in the stable and getting stuck) and some are adjustable, which is even better. The roller should never be in contact with the spine because this can cause permanent damage and a breast girth should be used to prevent the roller from working backwards. It is not necessary then to have the roller very tight. Some rugs have fitted surcingles and this is fine if the one nearest the withers is padded. One flat surcingle will neither keep the rug in position nor keep pressure off the spine, so these types are best unpicked. Your saddler, or even you yourself if you are good with a needle, can fairly easily pad a webbing roller for a tiny pony. Like a well-fitting saddle, you should be able to see straight along the spine of a roller, through to the other side.

A New Zealand rug is useful for protecting the pony from the elements when he is turned out to grass to relax during the season. Take care that the straps are cleaned and kept supple, and if the rug looks as if it might rub precious hair off the neck or shoulders, sew a piece of sheepskin round the neck to take off the pressure. If the weather is chilly, you might consider putting an anti-sweat rug beneath the New Zealand rug to trap a layer of warm air for insulation. Remember that sunshine can turn a New Zealand rug into a turkish bath, so watch the weather!

Tail bandages can be of the stockinette or elasticated crêpe variety and the main thing is that they should be washed often to keep them soft and stretchy. A tail bandage should be applied daily and not left on overnight.

If you have problems with a thick neck or jowl, you can buy proper garments to help swear off the fat. The jowl sweater looks very odd when the pony is wearing it and consists of a bonnet with two ear holes and a tape to tie under the chin. The neck sweater fits along and round the neck with tapes underneath to keep it in place. The sweaters are made out of heavy felt, topped with a moisture-retaining material to keep in the heat. It stands to reason that whilst the two items above can help remove fat, they cannot turn a naturally short thick neck into a long elegant one!

Headcollars come in a wide variety of styles. A good leather brass-mounted headcollar is a good investment and always looks lovely but the coloured lightweight nylon ones are very serviceable with the advantage that they are cheaper and scrubbable and come in a variety of colours.

Clothes for Travelling

Your pony can travel to the show in his usual rugs, depending on your transport, the weather and his temperament. If it is really

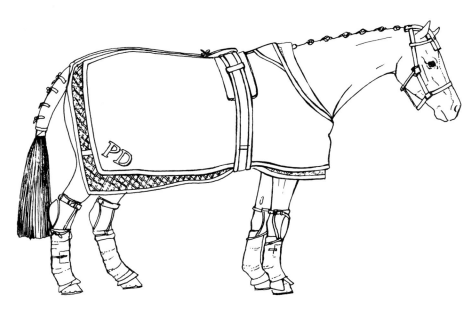

Pony dressed for travelling in cool weather

cold, his lined jute rug will be warmer than his day rug even if it is less smart. If your pony is used to wearing blankets in the stable, he will need them for travelling as well, especially if your trailer or horse box is rather draughty. However, if your horse box is a sumptuous affair, warm and draughtproof, or the weather is hot, beware of rugging too thoroughly and arriving with your exhibit dripping in sweat. Some ponies know when they are going to a show and get a little worked up. If you find that your pony tends to sweat during the journey, use an anti-sweat rug under his travelling rug. It will allow air to circulate and still keep him warm. You will also have to train yourself to arrive earlier to give the pony time to dry off.

Your pony will travel with his tail bandaged and perhaps popped into a nylon stocking to keep it clean. He will also need a tail guard to prevent him from rubbing and causing the bandage to slip down and ruin the line of the tail. This can be wool, bound to match the day rug, or in jute or soft leather. They have a long strap which buckles onto the roller and are tied round the tail with tapes, or in the case of soft leather guards, with buckles.

Most ponies travel in knee-caps because many an animal has

fallen down the ramp and broken his knees. They should be fitted correctly by buckling the top straps firmly and the lower ones loosely so as not to hamper movement. Keep the straps oiled and supple.

Travelling bandages should be used to minimise strain and jarring. They are made of wool and should be put on over gamgee tissue to minimise pressure and prevent stripe marks forming on the hair of the legs. You can use shaped quilted nylon ones which have velcro fastenings. They are washable and quick to put on and take off and come in colours to match most rugs. However, they do not give as much support as traditional bandages.

If the back of your partition is not padded, you might need to use hock boots made of felt and leather. Normally a show pony on the road would not wear more than this, unless he does alarming things like rearing in the box, in which case a poll guard might be a wise investment!

CHAPTER NINE

Grooming and Turnout

Judicious strapping can work wonders. It improves the coat and keeps the pores unblocked, thus promoting healthy skin. It stimulates the circulation and tones and firms the muscles. A good strapper can pummel off fat, develop muscle and do much to promote the good top line so necessary in a show animal.

After a few weeks in the stable, your show prospect will actually begin to look like one. His diet and exercise will be exactly tailored to his needs and as a result his bulges will be reducing and his weak parts will be starting to develop. What is more, his winter coat will be starting to come out. Resign yourself to the fact that rugs, blankets, stable and yard will be covered with a layer of pony hair which will permeate your house and your clothes, fill your vacuum cleaner, clog your washing machine, float in your coffee and, finally, block your drains. All this is worth while if at the end of it you can produce a pony with a summer coat gleaming like a newly shelled conker a week ahead of anyone else.

To this end, in your grooming-box (one of those large plastic shoe-cleaning boxes with a carrying handle is ideal), you will need to have the following equipment:

a dandy brush
a water brush
2 body brushes (1 soft, 1 medium), the leather-backed ones
   are best because, provided they are kept supple, they
   mould to the shape of the pony and do not clonk on the
   bony bits
rubber curry comb, or a rubber grooming mitt
metal curry comb (the rubber one will not get the hairs out
   of your brushes)
sweat scraper (or use the edge of your hand)
hoof pick (or 2). Attach a length of coloured twine to the
   end so they will not vanish into the bedding
2 sponges (one for each end)
2 stable rubbers (old nappies or thick tea towels will do)
piece of cactus cloth, old sacking, plaited wisp or rough
   towelling

101

pair of surgical scissors with rounded ends
large nylon comb for the tail (metal breaks precious hairs)
smaller nylon comb for the mane
plaiting thread, matched to the colour of the mane and a
    brightly coloured thread for practising
plaiting needles
3 tail bandages
2 large old bath towels
can hoof oil and brush or a Newmarket oiler
hoof varnish
medicated equine shampoo
2 lightweight plastic buckets
strong elastic bands
Bob Martins chalk block (only needed if you have a grey or a
    pony with white socks)
shoe whitener
large jar of vaseline
olive oil/coat gloss

The first priority will be to get rid of the old winter coat. You could clip it off and minimise the problem but I personally would not advise you to do so. The early shows are chilly affairs and clipped ponies tuck up and show their displeasure by misbehaving. I think a pony loses a lot of character when it is clipped and it does not suit the tinies at all. There is something very ponyish and endearing about a woolly coat which charms the judges far more than a shivering creature with its eyes sticking out of its shaved face like a startled whippet! There is also the fact that however hard you work on it, the coat never comes through as well after a clip. Nevertheless, some producers do clip their ponies, both before and during the season and also before Wembley. If you simply must clip your pony, let a professional do it first, whilst you practise on something else!

If your pony has a thick winter coat, as soon as it begins to move you can help it along with a rubber curry comb or a rubber grooming mitt. For a pony whose coat is not so thick, remove the loose hairs with a dandy brush and stroke out the hair with a household rubber glove. Rubber things work well on a loose coat because they have a slight gripping action. Bear in mind though that you are only encouraging loose hair to move – you are not plucking a turkey! An electric groomer (or a hand vacuum cleaner) is useful at this stage, but it won't help later on because it is no substitute for strapping.

When the coat has almost gone, and this can take several weeks, you will see that there are some long hairs left on the face, belly and the legs. You can hand-strip this. If they do not come out easily wait until the pony is just back from exercise and do it then. The pores will be open and you will not make him flinch, especially if you strip them a little at a time.

If there are too many to hand strip or they are very stubborn, singe them off with a taper, taking great care not to burn yourself or the pony. Thick whiskers must only be cut, never pulled.

Spend as long as you can spare on your strapping routine every day. First remove any loose hair from the coat with the dandy brush or the medium body brush, depending on the depth of the coat. Then take one of the body brushes to work with, making sure it is absolutely clean to start with, together with the metal curry comb. The type of bristled brush depends on the coat because the bristles must reach the skin, not just stroke the top hair, to be of any benefit at all.

Take the curry comb in one hand and, with the body brush in the other, start to work on the coat using short, circular and very energetic sweeps of the arm, putting your weight behind the brush and following the direction of the hair. Work quickly and briskly and after each few strokes run the brush over the curry comb (not the other way round or the dust will fall back into the brush). When you have cleaned the brush a few times, knock the dust out of the curry comb by tapping it on the floor.

This part of strapping is exhausting and if you do it properly it should make you sweat. Pay very special attention to necks and hindquarters and flabby parts, but go carefully on sensitive parts like the loins and head, the latter especially if your brush has a wooden back. Clumsy grooming can make a pony headshy. If your pony does not like brushes on his head use a damp sponge and a rubber to rub up his face instead, it will do just as well. Do not rattle the brush around his leg joints either or you will make him a fidget. Most ponies simply love being strapped and they will actually lean on the brush for you. Do maintain your basic discipline even in the stable. Train your pony to stand without being tied and to move a leg or himself over at a touch. He should not be allowed to wander round the stable just as he likes. It is important though that he enjoys his grooming periods and some grooms find that a transistor radio helps to keep both parties happy and relaxed – it certainly does no harm.

When you have spent as long as you can bear on the first stage, put the brush and curry comb aside for washing and take up the cactus cloth, sacking, wisp or rough towelling. Make it into a comfortable pad to fit your hand. Now start to bang away at the muscular parts, the neck, shoulders, rump and hindquarters. Work hard on flabby parts, soft fat and weak points that need building up. For this strapping to be beneficial you should be able to see the horse tense up his muscles in anticipation of your downward movement. It stands to reason that you should not bang any areas that are unprotected by fat or muscle. Avoid the loins and belly, the head and leg regions. If there are some rolls of fat you can pummel it with the edges of your hands to help break it up, rather like they do in a massage parlour.

Finally, take the stable rubber and polish the head and legs and finish off by rubbing along the lie of the coat all over until the coat is clean and the rubber is dirty. Damp the sponges and use one to wipe clean the eyes and nose, and the other to wipe the dock. If the pony is a gelding, wipe the sheath as well. He may be taken aback at first but he will soon get used to it. Keep your sponges separate and use one for each end only — having them different colours will help you to know which is which. As part of your daily strapping programme, pay attention to the mane, tail and feet.

Care of the feet is vitally important. A stabled pony should have his feet picked out at least twice a day and generally speaking, they should be oiled at least once a day. Many people oil the underside of the hoof as well as the outside. This does no harm provided that the feet are in good condition and are not too dry because oil excludes air and retards evaporation; more important it excludes moisture and to be in perfect order the underside of the hoof needs to absorb some moisture from the outside as well as from the blood. This can be demonstrated by the fact that a hoof can be half a size smaller after a dry summer than it was at the beginning. Sawdust and wood-chip bedding actually draw moisture from the foot which can become dry and hard, developing small cracks, flaking, causing the foot to lose its elasticity, and eventually affecting action. Therefore the foot needs access to moisture underneath for it to remain healthy. A pony that spends some time each day at grass will keep his feet naturally moist, and in a long hot summer (God willing) you can make some provision to soak the feet now and again, such as including in your exercise a shallow ford or a stream.

Moisture must not come from dirty bedding as this will cause thrush, an infection which occurs in the hollows between the frog and the sole, distinguished by its unpleasant smell. The natural varnish on the outside of the hoof helps to keep the moisture in the foot and for this reason the hoof wall should not be rasped. The application of hoof oil assists the natural varnish to do its job.

It behoves the producer of a show animal to find a good farrier and make a friend of him. A skilled man can do a lot to correct faulty action, to build up shoes and offset clips to disguise toes that turn in or out, to maintain feet in sound healthy condition and advise you on the best shoes for your pony. Most show ponies are shod with aluminium plates (alloys). They are very light and do not destroy natural action. Some ponies are better shod with light steel plates which wear better, and others, especially where the action is so exaggerated as to be almost comical, are better shown in ordinary standard weight shoes. Here again, each pony is an individual and his footwear must be tailored exactly to his requirements. A pony who does not move very well naturally can often be improved by shoeing with normal weight shoes and replacing them with alloys just before the show. This makes him feel light on his feet, but such practice is hard on the farrier and the pocket. The working hunter pony is almost always better shod with steel or ordinary weight shoes and they should have provision for a screw-in stud at each

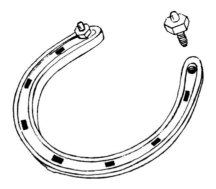

Studs for greasy going

outer corner which will help him stay on his feet on greasy ground during his jumping and galloping. You screw the studs in on the showground and remove them afterwards and they are also useful for exercise. Do not expect your pony to walk along any hard surface with studs in though; this is as bad as someone sending you out for a walk with a stone in each shoe! You can have more than one stud in each show and your farrier will advise you as to how many and which type to use.

Chances are that your pony's mane will be both too thick and too long. Quality ponies with a lot of Thoroughbred blood have fine manes which are easy to manage; but if your pony has a good deal of native blood he probably has a terrifying thatch of coarse, wiry hair. The only way to deal with something like this is to divide it into two separate layers, a lower and an upper. Brush half of the mane onto the wrong side of the pony's neck and secure this upper layer out of your way by using some strong elastic bands. Now you can get to grips with the lower half. Comb the hair and before you do anything make absolutely sure that the finished mane will hang on the correct side, which is the offside. When this is established, you can begin to pull the lower half of the mane until it is no longer than 5in (12.5cm) long. To pull the mane, take two or three hairs at a time, wrap them round your finger and tweak them out. If you pull the longest hairs first, you will thin and shorten at the same time. Mane-pulling should be done a little at a time: you should never try to do it all at once in one desperate performance. With a thick mane you can tweak away for days or weeks before you will see a difference but it pays to be patient. Ponies vary in their reactions to having their manes pulled. Some hardly seem to notice, whilst the ultra-sensitive types hit the roof if you tweak out a single hair. The best time to attempt it is after exercise, when the pores are open and the skin is warm and the pony relaxed. Any pony will become restless after a while, but if every grooming session includes a short stint of mane-pulling, pretty soon it becomes accepted as part of the routine. If the pony is one of the types who does not seem to notice the hairs being tweaked, guard against being tempted to tweak away for too long otherwise you will make him sore and the next time you come along, he *will* notice. Thoughtless pulling can give a pony a phobia about mane-pulling which is very difficult to overcome.

Bear in mind that the mane should be of equal length and

thickness all the way down the neck. Otherwise, when you come to plait you will start off at the wither end with neat little buttons, but by the time you get to the crest, your plaits will be more like tennis balls.

When you have really thinned out and shortened the lower half of the mane, you can take down the top. It is important to pull heavily from the bottom layer rather than the top because as the new stubble starts to grow it will stick up and spoil the line of the neck. The bottom stubble will not be so bad because it will not show so much and can be assimilated into the plait as it becomes longer and the new hair is pulled.

The top half of the mane should be shortened rather than pulled and this can be difficult to do if the mane is like wire. Far from hurting the pony, mane-pulling will probably cut your own hands to bits. A rubber glove or a strategically placed piece of sticking plaster will help. A lot of purists will gasp with horror if I suggest that you get the scissors or pocket trimmer out, but used carefully, pushing the scissors up the hair as you cut so that you do not get a straight line, you should be able to get away with it, and in a week or two you will not be able to tell the difference. With your scissors, you can also take 2in (5cm) of mane from between your pony's ears to allow the headpiece of the bridle to lie flat. Do not consider it if your pony has a lovely silky mane, but if he has a thatch, it seems a good excuse to get rid of a bit.

Likewise, if the mane tends to disappear under the pommel of the saddle, clip off a section up to a point where you want your plaits to begin.

After every mane pulling session, comb the mane through and lay it with the water brush. If your pony has one of those awkward manes that will keep flipping over onto the wrong side, put the offending bits into pigtails, securing them with rubber bands. This will help to train the mane to lie properly.

Now for the tail. Lift the tail by the end of the dock and shake it. Generally speaking, the hair that falls down on either side is the hair that you have to pull out. Obviously you do not pluck it all out, leaving bare patches on either side; you pull and shorten and train the remaining hair to stay flat and close to the dock by the use of a tail bandage. Again it is best to start pulling when the pony is warm and to pull a little at a time, making sure that you pull equally from both sides. Each time your have finished pulling a little, damp the hair and apply a tail bandage. Leave the bandage on for a few hours then grasp it with two hands and pull it down and off. You will be surprised what a difference it makes. Bandage down nearly to the bottom of the dock (see diagram) and do not leave a bandage on overnight as not only will it probably come off and get filthy and trodden on, but if you try to put it on tight enough to stay put it can cause the tail to be mis-shapen, make the underside sore, or kill hair growth. Beware of dirty bandages. They can cause soreness and infection. Keep yours soft and clean and stretchy by frequent washing.

Now and again one comes across a pony who really hates having his tail pulled. There is no reason why, with patience, he should not learn to put up with having a few hairs pulled out daily, but if you do not think you can cope, do call in an expert. An experienced groom from a show, hunting, or riding stable will accomplish the job fairly quickly and painlessly by getting someone who knows the job to button the pony down whilst it is done. This is unlikely to make it any easier for you next time though, and you might try to get an assistant to hold up a foreleg by the top of the hoof whilst you tweak out your daily dozen. Otherwise you may have some success from the other side of the stable door or some similar arrangement. If you do it often enough and reward the pony afterwards, he will probably get used to it eventually.

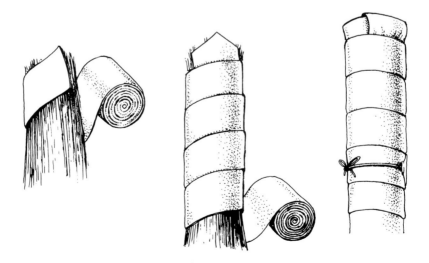

Tail bandage

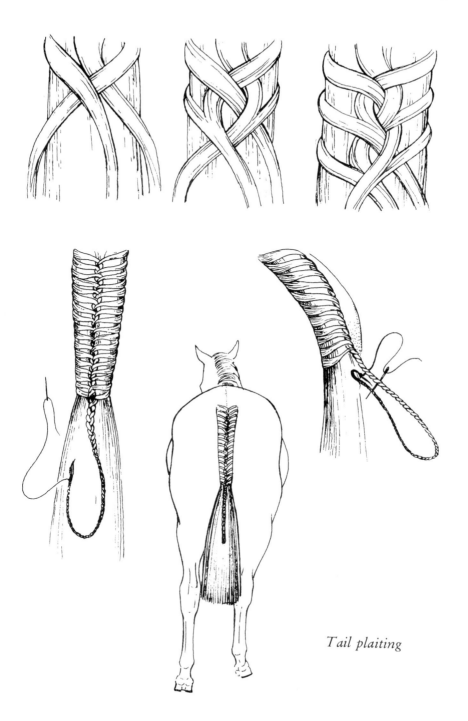

Tail plaiting

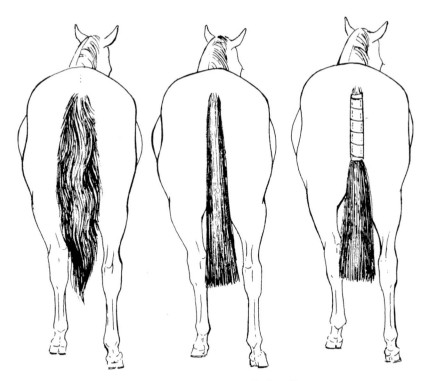

Natural and pulled tail

But if your pony is impossible (and you do not want to turn him into a kicker every time anyone approaches his tail), you could try showing him with his tail plaited instead of pulled. This is not strictly correct in a ridden class as it is more usual in the exhibition of breeding stock, but it can look very nice indeed if it is properly done. Plaiting a tail is not difficult, but it does take a lot of practice to achieve a perfect result. The diagram will show you how to go about it.

A very heavy, thick tail will need thinning all the way down because if it is bushy it will make your pony look as if he lacks quality. The tail should hang not more than 3in (7.5cm) below the hocks. If you cut it short your pony will have a cobby appearance and if you have it too long you will look as if you are trying to hide his hocks and the pony will look unbalanced. To get a tail to hang straight when it is carried properly, cut across sloping slightly upwards and inwards towards the hocks. Hold it firmly and snip at it until it is absolutely straight. Keep this clean line by snipping the edge every few days. Guard a thin, delicate tail with your life and never use a dandy brush or a metal comb on it. Brush it out very carefully with a nylon comb and body brush and in extreme cases, where the tail is very fragile, use a human hairbrush, a human shampoo and even a conditioner to prevent brittleness!

Native ponies often have quite a lot of hair on the legs and in the heels and this is known as 'feather'. You get rid of this by trimming. This can be accomplished with clippers (the small cordless type are ideal for use on ponies) but they do need a practised hand. Do not use them on wet, muddy heels or you will blunt the blades and cause the motor to overheat. Wash and dry the legs first and then take off the worst of the hair with the scissors; then you can clean out the heels and run the clippers up the back of the legs to make a smooth line. Do not clip off the coat, only the extraneous hair. Even so, the hair you have cut may leave underhair of a slightly different colour. This will soon blend in with the rest, but do not trim the day before the first show.

You can trim heels just as well with scissors and many people prefer to do so. Cutting close, clean out the heels, looking and trimming from all angles and taking lots of time to get a smooth outline. Next, run your hands up the back of the pony's legs and ruffle up the long hairs to make it easier to cut away. Cut upwards not across, so that you get a clean line and not steps. Be sure to use surgical scissors with blunt ends, not ones with sharp points which may stab the pony if he suddenly moves, and make sure that the scissors are sharp because blunt ones will pull the hair and upset him.

Trimming the head is obviously a delicate matter. Take care when using clippers on the head because if the pony jumps, you could cut off something you wanted to keep – not an ear perhaps, but a piece of coat which would leave a jagged mark. You may prefer to use scissors, hopefully allied to a steady hand and a calm relaxed pony. Take off any long hairs in the region of the throat to give a clean outline to the head. Look at the pony from all angles and nip off the hairs close to the coat. Trim off the clumps of hair sticking out of the ears and, progressing very gently, clean out the ears altogether. If your pony objects, and he is rather likely to do so at first, do a little each day until you gain his confidence and eventually you will be able to turn his ears inside out and he will not mind a bit. You can also trim the whiskers around the muzzle. If your pony is being shown off grass, do not clean the ears out altogether as the hair gives protection against weather and insects. You might consider leaving the muzzle whiskers intact also, as they do have some value as feelers.

If you are hoping to show in native pony classes as well as show pony classes (native ponies make excellent leading rein, first, and working hunter ponies with the added bonus that you can enter ridden native classes), you are expected to show 'au naturel', which means that you should not plait or trim, nor, strictly speaking, should you pull tails. You can get round the latter by plaiting the tail, but the first two are more difficult. If there is one thing I cannot bear to see it is 'show pony' turnout in the native classes and I think that you must make some effort to conform by unplaiting, even if you have to do a quick shampoo

In native pony classes you are expected to show 'au naturel'. Cantref Glory ridden by Andrew Cousins

job to get rid of the crinkles. It is easy if the native class is judged first, because you can plait afterwards.

Because your pony has clean heels and a short mane, you might lose a few marks for not being quite 'au naturel' enough, but you can cultivate a slightly rustic air by replacing your jockey's navy blue and velvet with a tweed coat and a bowler. You can also replace your coloured brow band with a plain one and cut out the fol-de-rols such as buttonholes and quarter marks. All this will help your exhibit to look at home in the class and he won't stand out from the rest like a child dressed for a party, or look as if he has wandered into the wrong judging ring by mistake!

If you are a novice producer, it will help to have a run-through of your pony's show morning routine. This will give you confidence and also allow you to fix a time-table for the show day proper.

First of all, sweep the stable floor clean, or do your preparation in a yard or stable with a clear floor. You do not want to be hunting through the bedding for lost items of equipment and more plaiting needles vanish that way than any other. Make sure that all your grooming kit is to hand and that your brushes and rubbers are clean. Dirty grooming kit puts back more dirt than it removes. If you have done your daily strapping well, your pony should not need any extra grooming. You might, though, need a small bucket of soapy water to remove any dirty patches. There are always more of these on show mornings but I have never been able to discover the reason why. Wash, rinse and dry the patches with the towel. Then brush the hair back in the right direction and let it dry naturally.

If your pony is shown off grass, or if he has a scurfy coat (check his diet if so!) you may have to wash him all over. Use a medicated shampoo. Wet him with warm water all over and apply the shampoo, rubbing him all over with the sponge. Avoid the nose, eyes and ears and be sure that he does not drink the soapy water whilst you are not looking. I had this happen once and it terrified me although the pony did not seem any the worse for it. Rinse all of the soap out thoroughly with buckets of warm water or, if your pony has strong nerves, a plastic watering can with a spray rose. Scrape off the surplus water with a scraper or, perhaps rather kinder to a tiny, with the edge of your hand. Chase the water off his legs by running your hands down them. Use a wet rubber on the head. When the surplus water has been dealt with, give the pony a good rubbing down with your old bath towels. Then make the coat lie properly by going over it with a clean brush, put a string rug or pack some clean straw under his rug, put on some soft stable bandages (make sure to dry the heels first), and then give the pony some gentle exercise in hand or on the lunge until he is dry. The important things to remember when bathing a pony are that he should not get chilled or have to wear damp rugs. If you do not have a spare rug to pack with straw, use sacking or a spare rug with a roller on the top. Of course, if it is a nice hot day, the pony will not need as much wrapping up; he will dry off naturally if you tie him in a sunny spot out of any draughts. Bear in mind that a pony who is being shown from grass cannot be subject to the same rigorous grooming programme because it is essential that the coat is allowed to retain natural oils. You must groom lightly, finishing with a soft damp body brush to remove surface dust and wipe with a cloth to polish.

With the coat dealt with, you can turn your attention to other things. Pick the feet out into a bucket. If you do not use a container, you can guarantee the pony will pick up the dirt again. Scrub out the feet and, again, dry the heels. Cracked heels are very common and take a long time to get right.

Wash the tail if you did not have to wash the pony all over, in which case you will have done it already. Provided that the dock has been sponged, there is no need to immerse the tail beyond the end of the dock and this will help to keep your tail bandage up. Use a shampoo and add blue-bag to the rinse if your pony has a white tail. Whirl the end of the tail to spin it dry. Damp the dock, add clear setting gel if necessary, and apply the tail bandage, keeping it firm and making sure that the tail hair is kept absolutely straight. You do not want to see any unsightly ridges when you pull it off later on. If a light tail needs protection against soiling in the box, pop it into an old nylon stocking (or half a pair of tights). Otherwise you can carry on bandaging right down to the bottom of the tail which looks odd but serves the same purpose. If you have a tiny native pony or want to make more of a very thin tail, you can obtain a crinkly effect by plaiting the tail from the dock to the end and securing it with an elastic band. Later on, you will get a fuller effect when you brush it out before going into the ring.

You can practise tail-plaiting at home but on the day you

might prefer to plait on the show ground because of the problems involved in protecting a plaited tail in transit. You can put a bandage and a tail guard on a plaited tail and sometimes it will stay neat, but often it does not so this is trial and error. Even if you plait on the ground though, do bandage and guard the tail for the journey. Neat, straight, flat hair is very much easier to plait than an untidy bush.

Whenever you practise plaiting, either mane or tail, use brightly coloured thread instead of the matching thread you will use on the show day. This is because it is easy to see and when you cut the plaits out there is less danger of cutting hair as well as thread.

Mane-plaiting is an art in itself. If you are inexperienced it will be easier if you break or cut one of your nylon combs to the appropriate size and use it as both comb and measure, so that all of the finished plaits will be the same width. Divide the mane up into the number of plaits you require and anchor each plait with an elastic band. This allows you to plan the number of plaits exactly and you will not get the next lot of hair mixed up with the piece you are working on. The traditional number of plaits is seven plus the forelock. This suits the working hunter pony very well, but for the ridden show ponies the number of plaits does not really matter at all. It depends on how many suit the pony and you can have as many plaits as your pone's mane will conveniently go into. Leading-rein ponies often have rather a lot of small button-like plaits to complement a dainty turnout. Larger ponies have slightly fewer, larger plaits, but they are still more elegant than the 'hunting plait' of the working hunter pony.

To plait a pony you need water, sponge, thread, needles, scissors, comb, and perhaps something to stand on to reach the forelock. You can use a clear setting gel on an unwieldy mane. Starting at the poll, remove the first elastic band from the measured piece of mane, damp and comb the hair. Now plait the piece firmly right from the top and as far down as you can go. Without letting go of the end, sew it up firmly so that none of the hairs can escape. Turn up the spiky end and wrapping the thread around it, sew it under so that you are left with a clean, neat, tight plait with a folded end and no loose hair sticking out. Now roll the plait under nearly until you reach the neck and you cannot go any further. Pass the needle through the roll a few times to secure

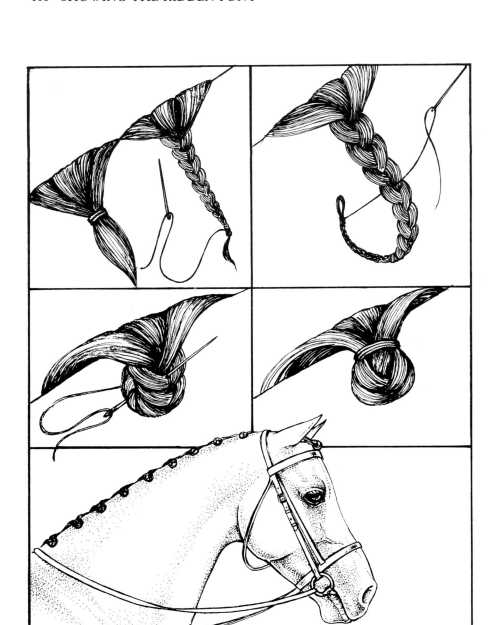

Plaiting the mane

it and collect any stray hairs on either side of the plait by taking the thread round the plait before finishing off. That is really all there is to it. If there are any bits sticking out from the plait, it will not hurt to nip them off to achieve a neat, hard outline.

As you progress down the neck, check that the plaits are level and even-sized. If some are much thicker but of an even width to the rest you will have to pull the mane a little more to thin it. When you have finished you may find one plait needs to be re-done because you have started plaiting from a slightly different angle. Practice will get it right every time. Angle-plaiting can help minimise a thick neck and make more of a poor one. For the latter, hold the hair up in the air as you plait so that the finished plait sits almost atop the pony's neck; for the former plait as near vertical as you can so that when the plait is rolled under it sits under the neck with no part of the mane visible from the other side.

On the day of the show, you may like to plait up most of the mane before you set out and finish it off at the show. Most people leave the forelock and the last few plaits at the wither end until the very last moment. This is because if the pony is allowed to eat hay during the journey, he can fill his topknot with seeds, while the rug will probably rub the lower plaits, or worse, the pony can pull out hairs simply by stretching out his neck if you plait them too tightly and these last few plaits can be pathetically thin by the end of the season. I would not really recommend leaving a pony plaited all night because not only will the plaits become uncomfortable and cause him to rub at them, but he can fill the plaits with seeds, dust or shavings if he is bedded on them. If you really must leave a pony plaited for a longish period it will probably pay you to make a little linen hood, tied with tapes, to keep the plaits clean.

Your pony is now ready to be dressed for travelling, but if you are just practising, you may as well go the whole hog and finish off by doing the things you will have to do at the last moment, just before the pony is due in the ring, preferably when he has had all the schooling or warming up that he needs. The first thing to do is to finish off the plaiting. Check the plaits for firmness and tweak out any loose hairs. Give the pony a brief grooming with a soft clean brush and follow this with some brisk work with a rubber. Rub him up everywhere, paying particular attention to the fiddly bits like elbows, jaws, legs and ears. A well-produced

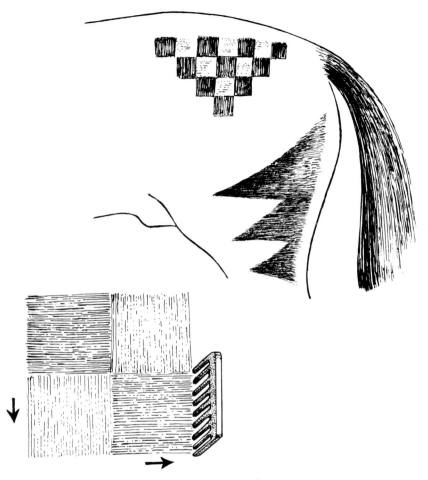

Quarter marks

healthy pony should have enough natural shine, but some coats do benefit from the discreet use of a spray-on top dressing. If it is fly weather, a little repellent wiped over the coat on a cloth will keep them at bay while a dull and dusty coat may respond to a wipe with a paraffin rag but do not smoke whilst you are applying it!

If you like to have quarter marks on your pony's rump, now is the time to apply them. Quarter marks are made by pulling the coat against the lie of the hair with a small-toothed piece of comb. You can make a chess-board pattern if you have a geometrician's eye for accuracy, or you can buy stencils to make the job easier. You do need a pony with a fine coat for them to look good, and you can help set them by using a burst of hair lacquer as long as your pony does not have a fit when you try it! You can make dragon's teeth on the flanks with a body brush by slanting the sweeps of the brush towards the tail, difficult to describe but actually quite easy in practice. Take care not to emphasise weak points. Practice at home and be totally objective. If in doubt, leave quarter marks alone. As a general rule, quarter marks are out of place on the working hunter pony.

Next, pull off the tail bandage and gently brush out the bottom of the tail, removing any hairs which fall below the clean-cut base. Check that the dock, eyes and nose are clean, and with your pot of vaseline touch up these hairless areas to highlight them. Smear your palms with a little olive oil and pass your hands over the dock and rub gently through the tail. The trace of oil left on your hands can highlight hocks and knees. Don't overdo the oil or you will end up with a greasy coat and don't use oil if you are showing on a dry, dusty ground. Now take your chalk block or talcum powder any white socks or stockings. It is best not to chalk on the face because it does tend to come off onto tack and attendants. A dull star or socks can be brightened by a dab of tennis-shoe whitener, brushed lightly when dry to separate the hairs.

Some producers use greasepaint to enhance faces but this should be used with restraint and practised at home. Like make up, one should not notice it, only the effect!

Lastly, check that the feet are picked out and clean, and varnish them. Some producers have their own special polishes, one of which looks to me to be suspiciously like grate blacking! I am sure this does not do any harm as long as it is scrubbed off later. The trouble with oil is that it gathers dust, while hoof varnish – available in black, brown and clear – stays on and on and builds up on the hoof. It does look good though.

The only thing there is left to do now is to saddle the pony and put the jockey on the top. It stands to reason that you will check them both over very carefully before you send them into the ring. Make sure the girths are tight and that the stirrup leathers are not twisted. Look at the pony from the front and make sure that his noseband and browband are straight. Brush any hairs off the jockey's coat and rub up his boots, even the soles. Is the hat straight and well brushed and the hair tidy? Have you used tape to tie on the number, is it the *right* number and the correct way up? Are the pockets of the coat bulging with unnecessary items? (All the jockey needs is a handkerchief and the pony's BSPS registration card together with his own BSPS membership card and a Qualification card if necessary.) Have you checked to see if you need to display a white arm-band to be eligible for any special award? If all these things have been successfully accomplished, you can relax and save your nerves for the real thing!

CHAPTER TEN

Ringcraft

When your pony and jockey are ready for the ring, it is a good idea to start them off gently at a small local show in a friendly, low-key atmosphere. The small gymkhana probably will not have a class for ridden or working ponies as such, but is sure to have a class for the best turned-out rider and pony and this should be your aim at first. It will test your production and it will introduce your pony and jockey to the ring with the minimum of stress because the ringcraft required in such a class is minimal. You can also test your combination in 'Best Rider' classes which will be more demanding for your jockey, and prospective working hunter pony champions should not scorn 'Handy Pony' and minimus jumping because every scrap of ring experience helps to bring pony and jockey on. When you are winning regularly at this level, it is time to move up a peg.

Classes for ridden ponies above gymkhana level are very likely to be affiliated to the British Show Pony Society, which means that ponies exhibited in them must be owned and ridden by members of the society. Membership, then, is essential before you go any further, and a close study of the society's rules is a priority. Not only do you have to join yourself, and your jockey, but your pony must be registered with the society on an annual basis. He will also have to be officially measured by the Joint Measurement Scheme to ascertain that he is within the height limit for the class in which he is to be exhibited. The JMS operates from the British Equestrian Centre and it acts on behalf of all societies whose members exhibit or compete in events divided into sections by height, measuring anything from a show-jumper to a Shetland.

To have your pony measured, you apply for a JMS county-by-county list of veterinary surgeons who are appointed to the panel of official measurers. Then you ring the nearest and ask him to measure your pony. This will be done promptly and you should present your pony unshod on a hard, level surface. A pony is measured annually until he is six years of age, after which he will be given a Life Certificate.

Affiliated shows are larger and (generally!) better organised than local events. The judging will take place in a good-sized level ring and the judge will be a member of the BSPS Judges' Panel which means he will be a person with many years' experience in the pony world and he will know exactly what to look for. Entries for affiliated shows have to be made weeks before the show on special forms sent to you with the schedule. At the larger, county shows, a catalogue will be sold on the show-ground giving details of all the classes and of every animal entered. Therefore you will be expected to supply information which will include the sire and dam of the pony, the breeder, stud book number, and its age and colour. You will also be asked for details of your jockey which are not as searching. If your pony is not registered in any stud book this will not matter at all because the information regarding the parentage is only really relevant to the breed enthusiast.

Every spring, the horsy press bring out their annual show issues, carrying a directory and calendar of shows for the forth-coming year. You will find this useful for planning your showing programme because it is possible to send for all the likely schedules in advance, using the directory of show secretaries supplied. Some shows will proclaim themselves as 'Qualifiers'. Applied to the riding pony classes in the 12.2–14.2 hands range, this means that the first prize winner in each height section will qualify for the Horse of the Year Show in October. Applied to the leading-rein, first-ridden and working hunter pony classes it means that the first prize winners qualify for the BSPS Championship Show at Peterborough in September. Naturally there is always very hot competition at a qualifying show because everyone wants a place at one or the other to crown their season.

Other important shows, like the Royal International, stage qualifying rounds for their ridden pony classes which would otherwise be too heavily subscribed. Details are given in the schedules of the shows concerned. For the largest shows your pony will need a valid 'flu vaccination certificate.

If your pony is a novice three year old, you will not be able to exhibit him until on or after July 1st in his first season. A novice pony is one who has never won a first prize valued at £5 or over in the 12.2–14.2 ridden pony classes at the start of the season and all novices must be shown in snaffle bridles. Not all shows put on classes for novice ponies so your choice will be rather more limited. There is nothing to prevent you from entering your novice pony in open classes and some shows do offer a special prize for the best novice pony in the class. A novice pony must be four years old to be eligible to compete in an open pony championship and he may go forward in a double bridle. Obviously you would only consider putting your novice into open competition if he is really outstanding and able to hold his own. There is no point in entering a pony who is going to be hopelessly outclassed.

From the very start of your showing career it will be helpful if you keep a show diary. As well as keeping a record of show dates and entries, you should make notes after every show which will help you to plan your showing programme the following season. Information on judges preferences, show routes, their shortcomings and inconveniences, dates of trophy returns etc., all these things will be invaluable when you are faced with piles of schedules next spring.

Primary Considerations

The care of the pony in transit is very important if he is to arrive at the show in the right frame of mind. On a long journey with a novice it might be wise to take a break half-way to give limbs a rest, to offer water, and if necessary a small feed. If you can find a suitable spot, it may be possible to unbox the pony and let him walk about for a while. This is especially important if you are travelling him in a trailer or a box with poor springs. Travelling is tiring and constant jarring and the strain imposed by cornering can spoil a pony's freshness and action. Boredom can also turn a pony into a mischievous passenger! One showing stable has installed piped music especially for the ponies in transit and maintains that they love it.

You will obviously know if your pony loads well, and will not leave it until the morning of the show to find out. Good loading is a matter of patient training. If you have difficulty, park your box or trailer in a handy spot and give your pony loading lessons every day as part of his basic education. Be satisfied with even slight progress and be sure to reward every forward step. You can have an assistant to give gentle encouragement from behind but on no account should the pony be chased in. Some days there will be no progress at all with a problem pony and the whole exercise will seem to be a complete waste of time but eventually, even if it is only out of boredom or curiosity, the pony will take another step. When you progress up the ramp and into the box, be sure the pony does not run backwards again by slipping a bar or breeching-strap across. Then you can give the pony a feed. If you leave a small feed in the box every time you load him, pretty soon you will find the pony will be leading you up the ramp. Patience and training are the only answers for problem loaders and lost tempers and fights will only make the pony fear the box or trailer more than ever. Discipline is quite another thing and if an experienced pony plays about, give him a sharp reminder by all means.

Take enough food for the day and water for the journey as there is usually provision for fresh water supplies on the ground. It may be a good idea to carry a little more than you need in case of break-downs. Grass ponies must be fed cut grass otherwise they look hollow. Cut your own at home if they are stabled the night before. Large shows where there are native classes will often provide cut grass, which should only be fed if it is cool and green and fresh. Alternatively, you will have to put on a head-collar and lead your pony out to eat as often as you can. Take spare rugs and bandages for use if the others get wet or damp. It will do your pony no good at all to travel in damp clothing.

If you need to stay overnight at a show, you can arrange to hire a temporary stable for your pony and you should arrange this at the time of entry. The stable will be a wooden affair, one of a row of stables with canvas or sacking to use as a top door. The floor in most cases will be grass, and straw is usually supplied as bedding. If your pony is not usually bedded on straw he may eat it and blow himself out like a balloon, so arrange to take your own peat or wood chips instead. You will also need to supply water-buckets, portable mangers and hay-nets.

If you intend to spend a lot of time at shows, it will make life a lot easier if you can do it in a reasonable degree of comfort. For casual showing, a couple of folding chairs, a table and a gas-ring to boil a kettle will be enough, but for anything more ambitious, a horse box with some kind of living accommodation is a godsend and if you have very small jockeys, a portable loo is very useful since showground loos vary in their accessibility and standards. Many professional showing people and dedicated amateurs hitch a small caravan onto the back of the box and you can imagine how much easier life suddenly becomes. It is perfectly possible, though, to manage without such plush facilities and many people manage without, spending the occasional night with a camp bed and sleeping bag in the back of the trailer or box.

If you have a novice or new pony, you will not have any previous showground experience to guide you as to how much pre-class preparation your pony needs. If your pony is a novice, it is often a good idea to take him to a few shows simply as a spectator, so that you can gauge his reactions. Some producers take their youngsters around with them for perhaps half a season until shows become routine. Many an owner, sending his pony to be professionally produced, has been astonished to see his pride and joy being used as little more than a bicycle between box and ringside but this stands the pony in good stead when its time comes.

Generally speaking, a good basic routine is to lead the pony out first in a headcollar to let him assimilate the sights and sounds of the showground. Afterwards you can give him some gentle lungeing, in tack, to induce calmness and obedience, followed by some steady schooling in a fairly thinly populated area of the ground under saddle. There can be no hard and fast rule however because the time for this depends entirely on the pony. If he takes a long time to settle he will obviously need longer than a pony who loses his sparkle rather quickly. Ponies vary enormously in their requirements, some will not give of their best without being worked for an hour or even two, before the class, and some do not perform at all unless they are taken straight from the box to the ring. After a few outings, you will be able to decide what is best for your pony and organise a routine and a timetable. If you are starting your pony off indoors (or qualify for the International or Wembley), be sure to give your pony and jockey some practice in an indoor school, taking your own music and audience if possible! So many ponies throw away their big chance because they are totally overwhelmed and disorientated by an indoor arena.

The Riding Pony Class

Having prepared the pony and child for the ring and ascertained that your class is running to time, present yourself at the appropriate place and let the child and the pony walk quietly round the collecting ring until the class is called. Do not jostle to get your exhibit into the ring first. Hang back until almost all the class are

Do not jostle to get your pony into the ring first

in and send your exhibit into a good space when the initial rush is over. Getting space for the pony is a thing that your jockey must learn by experience. He must learn to use his head and not allow the pony to be blocked from the judge's eye by others, or stuck in a bunch of ponies so that free movement is restricted. After a while your jockey should find and keep a good place by instinct and if he sees the space becoming crowded, he will either pass other exhibits (on the inside and fairly swiftly so as not to 'block' them) to a better space ahead, or ride a small circle and fall neatly into a space behind.

When the ponies enter the ring, the judge will allow them to walk for several circuits to enable the steward to check that all the exhibits are forward, and to form those valuable first impressions. If the pony needs a little encouragement, the jockey can use more outside leg but he must not, in his anxiety, hurry the pony along or cause him to break into a trot. A good rhythm should be maintained. Whilst keeping half an eye on the judge, the jockey should also be aware of the steward who will be positioned nearer to the ponies in order to give them the signal to trot as they pass him. When the jockey sees the first pony trot, he must be prepared. The transition from walk to trot should be smooth and unhurried and the jockey must not lose his head and let the pony speed up because he is being passed by ponies going too fast, or showing extension. So often one sees the whole class battering round far too fast with the whole thing taking on the aspect of a race simply because the jockeys are not using their heads and presenting their ponies in a balanced, fluent manner. Space is more difficult to find and maintain at the trot because ponies move at different speeds and there is necessarily more passing going on. However, the judge will normally watch the ponies trot past him at a particular spot and it is up to the jockey to position himself well so that the judge has a clear, unobstructed view of the pony.

The same steward will give the command to canter. The jockey should keep the pony calm and balanced and see that the pony goes into the canter smoothly and quietly and on the right leg. If, in the excitement of it all, the pony sets off on the wrong leg, the jockey should bring him back to the trot with the minimum of fuss and try again. It is important that he and the pony should not become flustered. Correcting a leg is not a fault – failing to notice that the pony is on the wrong leg most certainly is!

At the canter, the judge may require to see the ponies going the opposite way. The steward will direct one of the jockeys to change the rein across the ring and the rest of the class should follow suit. Your jockey should trot across the ring for a short way and ask the pony to canter again on the turn onto the new rein as this will help to get the pony started on the right leg. To be strictly correct changing the rein also means changing the stick into the other hand, but this does not matter too much.

After the judge has seen the ponies on the other rein, the steward will give the command to walk. Teach your pony to make this downward transition in stages, canter to trot, trot to walk, so that the effect is gradual and smooth. He must use his legs to get good forward transitions, not allow the pony to flop back into the lower gait. The walk should be long, relaxed and fluent, rather than over-collected with a chopped stride, the latter caused by nagging heels and a heavy hand.

The steward may ask the ponies to make a smaller circle around the judge to enable him to make a selection for the

People get terribly strung up about showing – a study in concentration, not only in pony and rider but also in every single person at the ringside

preliminary placings. Then he will call the ponies in, one at a time. The jockey should keep an eye on the steward, watching for his turn and when he is called in he should take care to stand the pony in line with the rest, leaving space enough between his neighbour for the judge to walk without danger to life and limb.

When all the ponies have been placed, there may be two lines of ponies, a front and a back line. The judge will walk down the line of ponies to assess them individually and he may have a word or two with the jockeys, asking a question about the pony's age or breeding. The jockey should be informed enough to give the relevant details but chatterboxes should be discouraged from launching into a story of the pony's entire career.

In line, the jockey should make sure that the pony stands up properly and does not nod off. To be sure that the pony is standing correctly it should not be necessary to swing down and look. The jockey can see by the shoulders which leg is in advance of the other, and he will develop a 'feel' from the saddle for a trailing hind leg. A tap with the cane will bring it under if the producer has done his homework.

After the judge has inspected all the ponies, he may decide to send the back line out. Judges never like to do this but there is often a tight schedule to consider, especially at the larger shows. It can be a bitter blow to the producer and the jockey not to be given a chance to do an individual display, but it is something they have to learn to live with. Large shows are staged to entertain the public. Their very existence depends on the profit from their 'gate' and forty individual pony displays are not the best kind of spectator sport. So accept such happenings with good grace and resign yourself to the fact that one of the most important lessons the show-ring can teach you and your jockey is how to cope with disappointment.

When the first pony leaves the line to perform its individual display, your jockey should watch carefully, because although a display is fairly standardised, some judges do have their own ideas about what they like to see and get very ratty if the child does not do exactly as he is told. The standard display is for the child to ride up to the judge and stand the pony a short distance away so that it can be inspected. The pony should stand up properly and when the judge has looked at the pony he will give the signal, a word, a nod or a smile, for the display to begin.

Normally this entails a walk to the perimeter of the ring, a trot of one circuit, followed by a figure eight at a canter with a simple change of leg, finished off with a short burst of a gallop down the far-side straight of the ring. The pony should then trot back to the judge and halt smoothly in front (but not too close) of him. This may be followed by a rein-back and a full halt with the jockey loosing the reins (but not dropping them altogether) to show that the pony is obedient and will not bomb off again. A girl should drop her head to the judge as a mark of respect and a boy should remove his hat. The judge will acknowledge the courtesy and the child will return to his place in the line. During the individual show it is obviously important that the jockey stays calm and does not try to rush the pony in his anxiety to have the display over and done with. The display should be smooth, unhurried and relaxed. So many children ride their ponies round as if they have a train to catch.

After all the individual shows, the judge will see some, or perhaps all, of the ponies with their saddles off. At this point you or an assistant must go into the ring to assist your jockey. You must be well turned out (with a hat for larger shows) and you should carry a skeleton grooming kit for running repairs. The pony should be unsaddled and the saddle put somewhere behind the line of ponies, out of the range of stray hooves. The attendant should rub up the coat where the saddle has been, wipe the pony over with a rubber and check the jockey for loose hairs and neatness. Side-saddle skirts should be hooked up on the button provided.

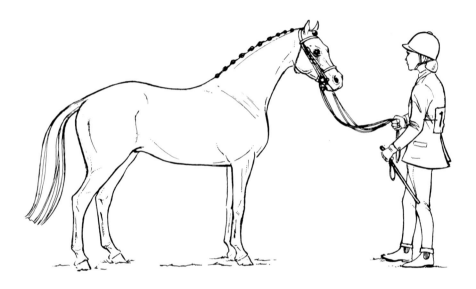

Your jockey should stand the pony up properly in front of the judge

When it is your pony's turn, the jockey should be ready to lead the pony out and stand him up properly in front of the judge. He will look the pony over, and walk round it and may feel the legs or neck, lift up a foot, and, if he is very thorough, look at its teeth. He may also ask the jockey a few questions. Then he will ask the jockey to walk the pony away and trot back towards and past him, so that he can see how well it moves. After this, the jockey returns to his place, the attendant helps him to saddle-up and mount, checks the pair over, and leaves the ring.

Finally, the ponies will be asked to circle the judge at a walk so that he can make his final selection. When the ponies are lined up in their order of placing, the prizes will be presented. Most ponies get to know when the class is over and the tension relaxes, but the jockey should not allow the pony to race out of the ring, or to misbehave when the winners are being applauded. Ponies not expected to perform a lap of honour should leave the ring quietly and if the opportunity arises, producer and jockey should offer a word of congratulation to the winners.

The former procedure for judging is also applicable to child's first ridden pony classes, with the exception that they are not expected to gallop, and they are not asked to canter as a class, only individually during their display. The Leading-Rein Class is judged as an in-hand class using the same basic procedure excluding the canter, and the individual show is restricted to a simple walk and trot. Side-saddle ponies and pairs of ponies are judged in exactly the same way as ridden ponies, but it is unusual to ask for the saddles to be removed in the latter.

Apart from the Intermediate class, none of the ridden pony classes is expected to gallop as a class, but the 13.2 and 14.2 ponies can be asked to gallop in fours at the judge's discretion. In the latter class, which is intended to act as a stepping-stone for teenage riders making the transition to adult showing classes, slightly more horsemanship and professionalism is required and the jockey must show that he has learned showmanship and ring-craft and has enough experience to really show a horse especially at the gallop. The transition from pony to horse is a difficult one and a large part of the difficulty is in learning to manage the confines of the show-ring at a gallop on a long-striding animal. The jockey needs to be able to slow up and balance the horse in order to ride the corners, and to be able to lengthen the stride and keep the horse straight along the rails, not allowing the horse just to fly round in a circle, ignoring the corners, falling inwards at a flat-out pace all the way round, like a motor cycle on a circuit. All this can be learned in the Intermediate classes before taking on the professionally dominated adult showing classes.

The Working Hunter Pony Class

The judging of working hunter ponies is more complicated because it is judged in two separate phases. Phase one is the jumping and there will normally be a draw for the order of going and this will be posted in the collecting ring so that you can organise your pony and jockey and have them warmed up, practised as necessary, and ready for their turn.

We have gone into the course and the type of riding it requires in Chapter 6, but the method of judging the class is as follows. Penalties for jumping faults in the first phase are awarded as follows:

Knock Down	10
1st Refusal	15
2nd Refusal	15
3rd Refusal	Disqualification
Fall of pony or rider	20

In addition to this, every competitor starts with 50 jumping points, from which the penalties above are deducted. The judge also has a further 10 points out of which he will award a percentage for style and manners during your pony's jumping round. Thus, if your pony has two fences down, and the judge awards 8 points for style and manners, your pony would finish with a score of 38 points at the end of the first phase.

Phase two is the showing section, but if your pony was eliminated in the jumping phase, he will not even be called for it. Normally, the only ponies called are those who have jumped clear but if clear rounds are rather thin on the ground, the next best will be called as well. If the show is operating with two judges, one judge will oversee the jumping phase and the second will judge the pony for phase two immediately afterwards. Here, the judge has a total of 40 marks to award at his discretion, made up as follows:

Conformation and freedom of action	30 points
Manners	10 points

As regards the exact nature of what your pony will be expected to do for phase two the only thing that can be said with any certainty is that anything goes! Judges vary enormously in their requirements and your combination should be prepared for anything. Possibly the judge will require a simple individual display, including a really good gallop which should not be a show pony 'burst' but a good low lengthy effort down both lengths of the rails, slowing up in order to take the corners in a balanced manner to demonstrate control. Possibly the judge may require a figure of eight and a rein-back, although this is by no means always the case. Almost certainly your jockey will be asked to run the pony up in hand with the saddle off. This should be accomplished with the minimum of fuss; no attendant is usually required to assist, but be prepared just in case.

If there is only one judge, the second phase will run after the jumping has finished and all of the ponies will probably be asked to enter the ring together. They may be asked to perform as a class but they are only allowed to gallop in fours to avoid the danger of a stampede! Many judges prefer this method as a pony being ridden in a class of others will soon show whether or not he tends to hot up in company, whereas most ponies can manage a steady display if they are performing alone. Often the individual display is dispensed with as such, and only used as a last resort when the judge has two ponies with the same score and little to choose between them. It will be seen from the foregoing that the working hunter pony needs a very thorough basic schooling and the jockey needs to be familiar with the basic technique of showing on the flat in order to be able to answer the requirements of different judges. At some time in the future the judging of phase two may become more standardised, but the present system, though confusing at times, does keep the jockeys on their toes and makes a welcome change sometimes to the clockwork standardisation of the riding pony classes.

At the end of phase two the judge (or judges) will confer and in due course the final scores and results will be announced. The ponies concerned, if they are not already in the ring, will return for the prizegiving. Exhibitors are perfectly entitled to ask to see their marks and some enlightened shows post them up.

Whichever class you have exhibited in and however well or badly you have done, care for your pony afterwards. Take off his tack and groom lightly under the saddle and round the head to prevent rubbing in the box. Cut out the plaits very carefully, taking care not to clip any hair along with the thread, and brush out the mane really well for the same reason. Put on the pony's rugs and bandages, offer him water, then leave him to relax for a while with a hay-net. Alternatively, lead the grassfed pony off to a quiet area to graze.

Sometime or other, you may find your pony being the subject of a random dope test, carried out on behalf of the BSPS. These are occasionally carried out at a major show and the pony selected is usually one of the winners. Drugs, whether used to tranquilise a fizzy animal or to disguise an unsoundness are a cheat and a disgrace and they are to be avoided at all costs. As defined by the BSPS, a drug includes any substance which might unfairly affect the performance or soundness of a horse or a pony. These include stimulants, depressants, steroids, tranquilisers, local anaesthetics, anti-inflammatory agents, including phenylbutazone, and masking agents. The dope test, though, is nothing at all to worry about (provided that you are an innocent party!). It merely consists of taking a sample of urine or droppings away for analysis. It is a wise precaution to take a sample for your own safe-keeping at the same time and keep it in your fridge (well wrapped!) until you receive notification that the test was found negative. In the event of the test being declared positive, if you were positively innocent, you would have some proof that samples had been mixed up somewhere along the way, and you would be able to challenge the analysis.

Take care also that any feed supplements you may be using do not contain any substance which will affect the result of a dope test. Check with your vet if you are in any doubt.

The last piece of advice I am going to offer to the novice in the show-ring is probably the hardest of all to follow. It is to enter into the spirit of showing with a light heart. It is not, after all, a matter of life and death. If your pony stands at the very end of the line or deposits your rider in front of royalty, it does not really matter all that much. It may sting at the time but later on, when you are more experienced, it will probably be one of your fondest memories. People get terribly strung up about showing. Unfortunately it tends to rub off onto the children and the ponies. Take a tip from the professional jockey and keep smiling, even when the most frightful things are going on underneath.

One of showing's great truths is that the novice years, when a yellow rosette won at a local gymkhana is a treasure beyond price, are the best. A lot of the fun has gone when you can only sit with clenched hands whilst your pony battles it out in silence for first place at the International; when it is a bad day if you are only reserve champion at the Royal Show. This was really brought home to me when, out of sheer inertia, I once sat through a programme about flower shows on the television. The interviewer asked one old gentleman, who had devoted his entire life to cultivating prize chrysanthemums, what he felt like after he had won the championship at the largest and grandest flower show of all. 'Laddie,' he replied, as he subsided onto a bench with his arms full of trophies and prize cards, 'I never want to see another . . . chrysanthemum as long as I live.'

Be warned!

Addresses

British Show Pony Society

Secretary (Membership)
Mrs J. Toynton
BSPS Offices, 124 Green End Road, Sawtry, Huntingdon,
Cambs PE17 5XA. Tel: (0487) 831376

The National Pony Society

Secretary (Membership & Shows)
Brook House, 25 High Street, Alton, Hampshire GU34 1AW

The British Horse Society
(the BSJA and Joint Measurement Scheme)

British Equestrian Centre
Stoneleigh, Kenilworth, Warwickshire CV8 2LR

Recommended Reading

The Art of Lungeing *Sylvia Stanier.* Excellent photographic guide. (J. A. Allen)

Constructing Cross-Country Obstacles *Bill Thompson.* Good tips for building jumps for working hunter ponies to school over. (J. A. Allen)

The Handbook of Showing *Glenda Spooner.* Excellent further reading on conformation with good clear diagrams and photographs. Useful chapters on natives, show organisation and classifications. (J. A. Allen)

The Horseman's Manual *Elwyn Hartley Edwards.* Invaluable book covering stable management, grooming, clipping, feeding, saddlery, ailments and schooling.

A Photographic Guide to Conformation *Robert Oliver & Bob Langrish.* The title says it all!

Riding in the Show Ring *Carol and Simone Gilbert Scott.* Clear and concise guide to dress, judging and classification. (J. A. Allen)

Riding Side-Saddle or Teaching Side-Saddle *Janet Macdonald.* Essential reading for anyone attempting to show or produce for side-saddle classes. (J. A. Allen)

Saddlery *E. Hartley Edwards.* Tells you everything you need to know about saddlery, including show tack and stable clothing. (J. A. Allen)

Teaching Basic Jumping *Martin Diggle.*
Teaching the Child Rider *Pamela Roberts.*
Useful for parents and producers anxious to train or improve their own jockeys. (both J. A. Allen)

Working with Hunter Ponies *John and Susan Thorne.* Comprehensive and highly recommended guide. (J. A. Allen)

Index

(Page numbers in italics indicate illustration)

Action 9, 36-9
  see also Dishing, Plaiting
Age classification of rider 20-7, 76
Attendant in leading rein classes
  86-7

Back 33
Back protectors 86
Bandages
  tail, 98-9
  travelling, 100
Barley 51
Benedict of Rossall 26
Bits 89-91
Blankets 95
Blagdon Gaytime 28
Bone 34-6
Boots
  hock, 100
  riding, 85-6
Bran mash 51-2
Breeding riding ponies 6
Bridles 65, 88, 91-2
British Show Pony Society 3, 5, 13,
  121
Browbands 90-1
Buttonholes 83
Bwlch Hill Wind 6
Bwlch Valentino 6-7
Bwlch Zephyr 6

Canter 66-7, 127
Cantref Glory 112
Cavesson 54-5
Cawdor Helen 82
Chest 32, *34*
Choosing a pony 16-17
Chop, Hay 50
Cleaning tack 95
Clipping 102, 111
Clothing
  riders' 79
  stable 95-8
  travelling 98-100
Coat *38*, 39, 102-3

Conditioning 43-53
Conformation 30-42
Cost of pony 16
Course building for WHP 13-15
Coveham Fascination 38
Curb chain *92*
Cussop Heiress 7

Dishing *36*
Display, Individual 69-71, 129, 133
Dope test 133-4
Double bridle 65, 91
Dress 79
Dressage saddle 94
Drop noseband 89
Droppings 52
Drugs 133-4

Eggbutt snaffle 88, *89*
Ewe neck *31*
Exercise 48-9, 54
  sheet 97
Eye 31

Farrier 105
Fat ponies 53
Feather 111
Feeding 50-3
  see also Fodder, types of
Feet 33, 44, 47, 104-6, 114, 119
Fences for WHP 72-5
Fencing 43
Fetlocks 33
Figure of eight 68
Fodder, types of 45
Forelegs 33-4
Friar Tuck 14
Frog 33

Gallop 67-8, 132
Gem's Signet 23
General Stud Book 6
Girths 91
Girthline 32
Gloves 86
Grassland management 43-4

Grooming 45, 101-20
  kit 101-2

Hairstyles 81
Hartmoor Silver Sand 13
Hats 79-81, 87
Hay 50
Head 31
Head carriage 64-6
Headcollars 98
Heels, trimming 111
Height classification 20-7, 76
Highway Code 49
Hindlegs 34
Hock boots 100
Hocks 34, *35*
Holly of Spring 5
Horsehage 50
Hunter Pony Stud Book
  Register 9

Insurance 42, 49-50

Jackets 83-4
Jodhpurs 84-5
Joint Measurement Scheme 5, 40,
  121
Jowl sweater 98
Jumping 10, 13, 72-6, 131-2
Jumps for WHP 72-5

Knee-caps 100-1
Knees 33

Leading 48-9
Leading rein ponies 17-20, *25*
  attendants 86-7
  bridles for 92
  classes 131
Lee Smith, Keith 12
Lennel Aurora 24
Lice 46
Limbs 33
Linseed 51
Loading for travelling 123
Lungeing 54-63

Maize 51

Mane
  plaiting 115-17
  pulling 106-7
Manners 19
Martingales 88-9
Mountain and Moorland Stud Book
  6
Movement 36-9
  see also Action, Dishing, Plaiting

National Pony Society 2-3, 6, 9
Native ponies 2, 6
  classes 112-13
Neck 31-2
Neck sweater 98
New Zealand rug 45, 47, 98
Nosebands 89, 92
Novice ponies 24, 123, 125
Numbers, class 86, 120
Nuts 51

Oats 51
Oiling feet 104-5
On the bit 64

Pageboy 11
Pairs of ponies classes 29, 87, 131
Pelham 89
Performance of WHP 12
Perry Ditch March Winds 84
Plaiting (action) *36*
Poll guard 100
Polo pony 2
Polo Pony Stud Book Society 2
Presence 39
Pretty Polly 4, 5
Purchase of pony 27-42

Quality 9, 23, 39
Quarter marks 118-19
Quarters 34

Registration papers 40-2
Rein back 68-9
Rider, show pony 78-87
Riding ponies 1-8, *25*
  classes 125-31
  height classification 20-6

saddlery for 91-5
shoes for 105
Ringcraft 121-35
Road safety 49-50
Roadwork 48
Rollers 97-8
Roughing off 53
Rugs 95, 97
  see also New Zealand rug

Saddlery 88-100
Saddles 90-5
Schedules, show 122
Schooling 54-77
  on the lunge 54-62
  under saddle 62-77
Schoolmasters 28
Shelters, field 43
Shirts 81
Shoes 44, 47, 105-6
Shoulders 32
Show hunter ponies 27
Show pony rider 78-87
Show saddle 93-4
Shows
  BSPS Peterborough 14-15, 122
  Horse of the Year 122
  Royal International 122
Side-reins 48, 55-7, 60
Side-saddle 28, 29, 87, 94, 131
Size 40
  height classification 20-7
  leading rein ponies 17
Small ponies' feet 47
Snaffle, Eggbutt 88, 89, 91-2
Snailwell Charles 37
Solway Sweet William 96
Spooner, Glenda 12-13
Stables 46-7
Standing still 71
Standing up 70, 128-9, 130
Stirrups 91
Strapping 101, 103-4
Studs, shoe 105-6
Sugar beet pulp 50-1
Summerhays, Reggie 22-4
Supplements, feed 52, 134

Tack
  see Bits, Bridles, Saddlery, Saddles
Tail
  bandage 98-9, 107-11, 119
  conformation 33
  guard 99
  plaiting 109-11, 114-15
  pulling 107-11
  washing 114
Teeth 46
Temperament 27-9
Thorne, Susan 9
Tonto 15
Transitions 69
Transport 123-5
Travelling 123-5
  clothing for 98-100
Trimming 111-12
Trot 37-9, 49, 66, 127
Trotting poles 66-7
Turnout
  of pony 101-20
  of rider 79

Vaccinations 53, 122
Veterinary considerations 39-42
Vitamins 52

Walk 37-9, 65-6, 126-7
Washing pony 113-14
Water 44-5 47
Whips 57, 86
Whiteman, Davinia 14
Winter feeding 45
Wintering out 43
Working hunter pony 9-15, 25, 26-7
  classes 131-5
  jumping 72-6, 131-2
  saddlery for 88-91
  schooling 71-7
  shoes for 105-6
Worming 44

Yeoland Foxglove 41